BY

 Published in the United States by Splatterbrain & Son, a charming publishing house based in Olde Spree upon Dingus.

ISBN: 0615574092
ISBN-13: 978-0615574097

THE AWESOME CONTENTS

When I wake up, my side of the trash heap is cold.

My quilt is missing. I lie there in the dark, rubbing my eyes, trying to think of where it could have gone. *I hope it didn't disintegrate*, I think. *After all, it's only some pieces of wet newspaper.* I reach out through the gloom, and find my answer: Pigrose, the disgusting little street urchin, has stolen it from me. Pigrose is also my beautiful little sister.

As I lie here, shivering in the cold, I am left with one thought: *Could life get any worse*? Actually, it could. Because all of a sudden, I remember that today is no ordinary day. Today could end my very existence altogether.

Yes, that's right. Today is the first day of school.

Oh, and it's also Reaming Day, when kids between the ages of twelve and eighteen are chosen to participate in the Hunger But Mainly Death Games, which, as you might expect from the name, is a tournament in which they fight to the death, and occasionally experience hunger. The children picked are called "sacrifices," and they are almost guaranteed to die in an excruciating manner. But the Reaming isn't till the afternoon. On a day like this, you've got to take things one at a time. Besides, I'm sure I'll never get picked.

But with all of this on my mind, I'm also sure that I won't be falling back asleep. I clamber out of bed, rubbing the sleep and trash out of my eyes as I stretch my toes in the glass-filled mud floor. I glance over at Pig, who slumbers on peacefully. Pig is twelve. In our world, that's considered old enough—old enough to starve to death, to kill and to be killed. It's also old enough to see R-rated movies, so it's not all bad, I guess.

But Pig is my little sister, and some part of me will always see her as a baby. I let her slumber on, and try to imagine what she's dreaming of. A warm bottle of formula? A new toy for bath time? A bright wooden block to bang up and down on the tray of her high chair? The inner workings of her baby-mind elude me.

Across the room, I can make out my mother's body curled up on a pile of old Styrofoam and greasy shirts. Fitting, the way she's claimed the best bed in the house for herself. Perhaps I should cut her some slack. She is my mother, after all. Then again, she's tried to bury me alive more times than I can count.

I stumble toward the shower and turn it on. When it's warm, I step in, trying to collect my thoughts as the garbage juice splashes over my long, brown hair. There's an old saying we have about garbage juice here: "It won't get you clean, but it probably won't make you any dirtier, and it might even knock off some of the old, dry trash that's stuck on you."

That's how things are in our region of Slum 12, known to most as the "Crack." Slum 12 is our nation's landfill, and the Crack is its most disgusting region. Any time there's a piece of trash that's deemed too gross to even be put in a landfill, it's smushed over into the Crack.

When I go downstairs, I see that Pig has left a present for me by the door. *How sweet*, I think, tearing off the bow. My jaw drops in horror as soon as I see what's inside: it's "cheese" from Acidbarf, the revolting and dangerous creature Pig refers to as her "cat." The cheese that dribbles from his four hundred pound body actually paints an accurate portrait of the creature himself: pitch black, oozing, and filled with semi-digested maggots. I'm repulsed by it, but I can't bring myself to tell Pig that. She loves Acidbarf too much. I'll never forget the day she brought him home: I was out front sweeping our dirt, when I looked up and saw Pig skipping towards me, with an unmistakably evil creature bounding towards her, about to tear her to shreds.

"Pig! Run!" I shouted, "MONSTER!"

"Don't be silly!" she called out. "This is my kitty."

"That is not a cat, Pig! THAT IS *NOT* A CAT!"

"Look! He's kissing me!" she exclaimed, as he batted her down and trapped her in his claws. "He's such a darling little—*OW*—fellow!"

I wasn't pleased by the thought of having another mouth to feed, and my body was already crawling with the ticks that dropped off Acidbarf's fur like dandruff. But when I looked into Pig's pleading eyes, I knew I couldn't disappoint her. And, to her credit, she's somehow convinced Acidbarf not to eat us. For our part, we pretend not to notice every time he drags the skinned corpse of a neighbor to our doorstep. Burying his kills in shallow graves, and not being eaten by him—this is the closest we will ever come to love. Which, from what I can tell, is how all relationships work, more or less.

Here in the present, the misery of my situation rushes back to me. I don't want to go back to school. Why do I even have to? Only a government as unjust as ours, which makes its own teenagers murder each other on national television, could cook up such a cruel form of torture. In some ways, I'd almost *rather* get stuck in the death tournament than sit through another school year. But we all know that's never going to happen.

I step outside and gently shut the door—an egg carton and a rubber band—behind me. Without warning, I get the feeling that this will be the last time I see my home.

And then I remember. Every morning after I leave home, we move to a new home. That's because our "homes" are actually piles of trash that either blow away in the wind or get picked up by the sanitation department—which, for some reason, exists in our town made out of garbage.

It's still a bit early, so I take my time and stroll through the streets. I pass the homes of the Crack's least fortunate, who are so poor that they must spend their entire lives in used graves. I pass the Crack's sole restaurant, a Little Caesar's. A shiver runs down my spine.

When I come to the entrance of the Trash Mines, I pause for a moment. Trash mining is the only way of life for most in Slum 12. It's hard work, and it can often be humiliating, since the Mines also function as the entire nation's sewer system. This is bad enough in itself, but the government makes things even worse by forcing every worker to wear humiliating signs on their chests: "I Love Doody!" runs a common one. Another,

"Today, My Breakfast Was a Doody." A third, "Stay Out of My Mouth! Precious Doody Treasures Inside For Me to Munch On Later!"

But if you're a diligent worker, you can make something of yourself. Maybe your supervisor will notice you, and give you some of those plastic rings that hold soda cans, or an old hunk of mayonnaise that's turned hard. My father was one of the best trash miners, or so I'm told. When he proposed to my mother, he was able to give her an engagement ring with one of the biggest mayonnaise emeralds the Crack had ever seen.

But if my father's story illustrates the glitz and glamour of trash mining, it also shows just how dangerous it can be. I'll never forget the day he was swept away in an underground poop river. The currents were so fast that not even his life preserver diaper could save him.

I'm headed to the woods that surround the Crack right now. We call them "The Tires" because, well, that's what they are—stacks upon stacks of old tires, in a magnificent array of sizes and types and states of housing rattlesnake families.

I tread lightly as I near the electric fence meant to keep us out. We are told the Tires are too dangerous for teenagers. They were closed off a few years ago after some kids found a stash of old fireworks, and burned their hands a little while setting them off. You wouldn't expect a government like ours to lose sleep over their subjects' day-to-day safety, would you? But it's another example of their infinite evil: they want to make sure that teens don't get to kill each other the ways they naturally enjoy, like playing with things that explode and driving cars fast.

I've come to the Tires this morning in search of Greta. Greta is my best friend and closest confidant. We look like siblings, what with our dark coloring and thick unibrows; and we act like the kind of siblings who are secretly dating—or, as they like to call themselves, "twins." Except that Greta and I are not in love. Not by a long shot.

What? Why are you looking at me like that? You think I don't know whether or not I'm in love with someone? Come on. Emotions and dating stuff can be pretty confusing, but give me credit when it comes to knowing my own mind. And it's not like every guy you're close with has to be a potential love interest.

Besides, Greta is great, but he's a little…extremely moody. Take my birthday last year. At the stroke of midnight, he appeared at my door.

"I wrote this poem for you," he said, shoving a piece of crumpled paper into my hands.

The world must burn.
Lava exploding into faces.
Their skeletons are screaming now.
No survivors.
-From, Greta.

"Oh…uh…wow…" I began.

"Don't bother thanking me," he said. "I just wanted to comfort you for being one year closer to the grave. Of course, I failed miserably, because comfort doesn't exist in this universe."

"Thanks all the same," I said. "See you at the fort?"

That fort is where I'm headed now. Greta goes there whenever he wants to think, or melt action figures. When I reach the ramshackle gate he's erected around it, I nod at the Greta's "sentry," and let myself in. It was a fun day when we found that cave with all the old skeletons.

When I come across Greta, he's hunched over something.

"Hey, Greta. Whatcha doing?"

He spins around in surprise.

"Bratniss!" he sputters, a brief flash of anger flickering across his eyes. "How many times have I told you not to question me about my dark experiments!"

"It looks to me like you're banging on some batteries with rocks."

"I wanted to see what was inside," he says. "Well, come on in…if you dare…"

I take a seat on a shower curtain, while Greta paces restlessly back and forth.

"Something wrong?" I ask.

"Not really," he says, "Other than the fact that for all I know, I'll be condemned to an excruciatingly painful death in just a few hours."

I stare at him blankly.

"Because I'll get picked to be in that death tournament."

I shake my head. Still nothing.

"Bratniss, I'm talking about the Hunger But Mainly Death Games!"

The Hunger But Mainly Death Games. Wow. I somehow forgot about them in the last few minutes. What's going on with me today? Whatever it is, it's probably another sign that I'm not going to be picked.

"Greta, there's no use dwelling on it," I tell him. "This is what every teenager has to go through, even if they live in some crazy alternate universe without death tournaments. Even then, the things adults do to them are just as bad. Like not letting them have co-ed sleepovers, or asking them to go get the mail."

"We could do it, you know," he says, pacing faster.

"What are you talking about?"

"We could jam a lightning rod into a barrel of toxic waste and put it in the graveyard and hope that it makes an army of zombies to kill the adults!"

"Uh..."

"Forget it!" he shouts. "It's obviously too deep and complicated for you to understand!" Then, with a flourish, he throws his black velvet cape across his face and turns his back to me.

"Have it your way," I say. "But come on, let's go hunt."

We walk out to the old hollow tree where we conceal our weapons. Which one will I use today? Bazooka? Anti-matter ray? Poison grenade launcher? Man, I love hunting.

All the weapons in the tree were my father's. He found them down in the mines, and taught me how to use them. He knew it was the only way to make sure I'd be safe from my mother if he died.

"Bratniss, before we start," he said on our first training day, "I want you to know that your mother loves you very much, in her own, special way. Unfortunately, that way is trying to murder you, because she's batshit crazy. So grab hold of this attack-chainsaw and let's begin."

To some, it might have been a sad moment. I was overjoyed. That may sound cold, but when I was a toddler, this was one of my lullabies:

Rock-a-bye, Bratniss, in your safe cage,
These bars will protect you when mommy's enraged.
If she should break through them,
Don't have any fear,
I made a machine that shoots tranquilizer darts at her if she gets too near.

Of course, hunting is illegal here. But if it's a choice between that and starving to death, I'll take hunting every time. Especially since starving to death is also illegal, and the punishment is "painful lethal injection." Anything that makes our capitol city, Big Huge Nice Capitol City, look bad is a treasonous crime. Even saying our country's name out loud is punishable by death: Pandumb. Sort of a crappy name, right? But the reason the Capitol (I'm just going to call it the Capitol from here on out, both for length-reasons and because not *every* name in a parody book can be a pun) chose it is all too clear, according to their Wikipedia page: *We, the most advanced city in the world, called on our greatest minds to devise the best name for our perfect country. If they chose something so remarkably stupid, imagine how dumb that makes you. You're so stupid that you would have probably called it Poopytown. Yep, that's how stupid you are. So obviously you're too stupid to ever stand up for yourselves or make us stop killing your children.*

"You know, all this talk of the Hunger But Mainly Death Games is making me wonder what it would be like to kill a person," I say. "I'm not sure I could do it."

"I have a feeling you'd be fine," Greta replies. "You just killed a family of squirrels with a single ninja star."

"But killing a person is different."

"You just picked up a venomous snake, swung it around to break its spine, and used it to lasso another snake, and now you're eating that snake raw."

True enough. But all the same, something inside me whispers that if I ever had to turn my mustard gas gun on a person, I simply wouldn't be able to. Mustard gas costs upwards of one wood chip. No way I'm paying that much to kill only a single human being.

After a while, we decide we've caught enough for one day. I look over my catches happily: I've bagged enough kills to keep my family eating raccoon gallbladders all winter.

And because today is no ordinary day, Greta and I decide to reward ourselves. Why not? We may never get the chance to eat an entire fresh hornets nest again.

"And may the odds—" he begins, mocking Pandumb's official slogan for the Games.

"—Make it true that when you're mortally wounded in an excruciatingly painful way, your body goes into shock and you don't feel anything as you die," I finish. It's not particularly encouraging, but it *is* realistic.

Before we head off to school, we decide to see if we can get anything for our haul at the Blob, which is a semi-conscious gelatinous creature that pulsates in the middle of the Tires. Nobody knows where the Blob came from. Some say it's always been there, at least since that chemical factory leaked into the Slum 12 retirement village. All I know is that when you leave a fresh kill on its membrane, sometimes it'll slide out a few gold coins. That happens about twenty-five percent of the time. The other seventy-five percent, the Blob shoots out hundreds of fanged tentacles and tries to kill us. But if you want to survive in the Crack, those are odds you have to take. There is no other choice.

I mean, I guess could always apply for a job at the supermarket. The starting salary for a checkout girl isn't half-bad. In fact, it's way more than I ever get from the Blob.

But that sounds way boring—*AAH TENTACLE*!

Twenty minutes and twenty narrow escapes from death-by-digestion later, we head off to school. On our way out, we make sure to say goodbye to Garbage Sally, the Blob's wife.

"See ya, Garbage Sally," I call out, waving at her floating figure, deep inside the Blob.

"*Heeelp*," comes her tiny reply. Greta and I chuckle. It's *so* Garbage Sally to joke around like that.

When we get to school, I notice a group of incoming freshmen clustered together, chattering nervously. Funny. When I was a freshman, I felt as if I had finally made it—as if I had become a *real* teenager, not just some kid who had celebrated a thirteenth birthday. But looking at this group, I'm astounded at how small they seem. Is that how *we* looked to the older kids when we were freshmen? Probably not. All three grades above us were born during famines, so they were much tinier and weaker than we were.

The bell rings, and we start walking towards the doors. That's when Pig catches my eye—and what I see makes my heart stop.

"PIG!" I shout. "PIG!"

She glances around as if she hears something, but she doesn't see me, and continues to walk towards the doors. I break into a sprint. I must do something, or it will all be over for her.

"Pig!" I exclaim, panting as I catch up to her just in time. "For God's sake, fix your hair. There's a weird chunk of it standing straight up."

There are some things I'll never get about little kids, and one of the biggest is why their hair sticks up in weird ways so often. It's like, four out of the five school days, they'll come in with one part of their hair defying gravity like it's tied to the ceiling. And next to it is a chunk that's matted down like oily beaver fur. I'm not criticizing them. It happened to me, too. I just don't know how it's scientifically possible.

"Bratniss!" she hisses, her face turning bright red. "You're humiliating me!"

"No need to get fussy. I'll use some of my mommy magic to get it down," I say, licking my hand and stretching it out towards her.

"Stop!" she cries. "I'm not a baby, Bratniss!"

I want to protest, but in my heart, I know she's right.

"Shoot, I'm sorry, Pig. It's just, you're my little sister. I guess I can be overprotective sometimes..."

Her frown begins to fade. Stepping forward, she wraps her arms around me and gives me a hug. I lean down to whisper in her ear.

"Now, I don't want to embarrass you in front of your friends. But do you want to do a quick diaper check before you go inside?"

"AAARGH!" she yells, breaking free of my grasp and running inside.

The rest of us file in slowly, under the watchful eyes of the group of insane murderers the Capitol uses as a police force—the 'Peace'keepers, a name so blatantly ironic that they added the quotes themselves. People say that in the Dark Days, our school was a maximum-security prison. Funny. Seems fitting, when you consider that both prisons and schools are known for serving sub-par food and having group exercise yards.

"All right, you worthless pieces of trash!" shouts a 'Peace'keeper as the thick steel gate clangs shut behind us. "Into your holding cells!"

A muscle-bound guard tosses me into the barbed wire enclosure that surrounds my desk. All around me, I hear the sounds of my classmates slamming into the rough floor, crying out in pain when they accidentally brush against the wire, that cursed devil's rope, the bane of our existence. I sigh. *Back to the grind.*

"Hey, Bratniss! How was your summer?" comes a voice to the side of me.

It's Magma, the daughter of Slum 12's mayor. Her desk enclosure is right next to mine. Though we occasionally talk, I wouldn't call her a friend. As the mayor's daughter, she leads a life of luxury I can scarcely imagine: clothes not made out of briers and tumbleweeds, a water source that only has a few dead horses in it. As a result, there's little we can connect over.

"Oh, pretty good. I found a new way to scrape rotting hunks of food out of deer intestines. It makes it a lot easier to dry the stomachs and make them into a tough jerky you can gnaw on while you're hunting."

From the look on her face, I can tell I've said the exact wrong thing. The barf that comes out of her mouth is probably another indication. I struggle to think of how to smooth things over, but never get the chance. The classroom door swings open, and in walks Ms. Woodruff. Tall, blond, and dressed in impeccably pressed rags, she cuts an imposing figure.

"Good morning, students. Let me be the first to say, 'Welcome back.' That, and, don't forget that talking out of turn will result in immediate death by sniper. Now, what do we say to the sniper for giving his time to help us learn?"

"Thank you, Mr. Sniper," we murmur.

"Have a good year, kids!" he replies with a cheery wave, up in his watchtower. I shake my head. How anyone can feel cheery on the first day of school is beyond me.

We start with history. I open my book to the first page. Like all pages of all schoolbooks in Pandumb, it is nothing but the sentence "Pandumb is great," over and over. I take out my pen and begin to carefully trace every word, as is required by law. Call me a nerd if you want, but it's sort of neat that to realize that by the end of the year, we'll have gotten through this entire book!

As we trace, Ms. Woodruff relates the history of Pandumb, which we've heard countless times. How it rose out of the ruined societies of the Dark Days to bring stability and prosperity to the entire continent. How eventually, the government realized that, instead of peace and stability, what people really like is evil and sadness and dying. How a group of traitors rebelled, lost, and were forced to send their children to a yearly death tournament as punishment.

But suddenly, for the first time, something about it seems strange to me. So, when Ms. Woodruff asks if anybody has any questions, I do something that no self-respecting kid should ever do: I voluntarily ask one. The class turns and stares at me (as best they can, anyway, since our neck shackles don't allow much head-movement).

"I don't get it," I say. "Why is that the only way?"

"I have no idea what you mean, Bratniss," she says.

"Wouldn't other ways work better? Like, what if they exclusively starved us? If that's all they focused on, we'd probably be much weaker, and just want to lie around on the dirt all day."

She shakes her head in exasperation. "You know as well as I do that scientists in the Capitol have proven that nobody *ever* rebels because of death tournaments. It's the Fifth Law of Thermodynamics, for crying out loud. And you know that the Rebels themselves agreed to the Hunger But Mainly Death Games when they were invited to help the Capitol draft a new Constitution."

"If that's the case, why are the parts the Rebels signed filled with written-down screams of torture?"

"That was back when pens became sentient for a little while. The Rebels were probably squeezing them too hard."

My blood starts to rise. This is too much! Not *every* adult can be as insane as my mom. Some of them must like their kids! And for them, the very idea of the Hunger But Mainly Death Games must be infuriating beyond belief! Especially that year when there was no food in the arena, and the only weapons were machines that let you make bacon from humans!

But there's no time to dwell on it, because then the bell rings and, *Woo-hoo! Half day!* We rush out happily and run down to the Square, where the Reaming is about to take place. I know it's stupid for us to be excited - we're all aware that all half days, like snow days, end in utter misery.

When we reach the Square, we break out into groups and have to try to assign ourselves to the correct holding pen in order of birth month, all without speaking. Then we have to get in a circle and hold hands with people across from us in such a way that we form a "human knot," which we then have to untangle from without letting go of each other. Neither of these have anything to do with the Reaming—they're just stupid team-building games the government makes us play in an attempt to calm us down, so that the Square isn't flooded with nervous pee. After that, the Mayor takes the stage.

"Good afternoon, citizens," he says solemnly, looking out from the podium in his most formal full-body Uggs. "Today, we celebrate Reaming Day, which is sure to become yet another shining mayonnaise emerald in the exquisite diadem that is Slum 12's history. As is customary, I will now read a list of your fellow citizens' greatest accomplishments in the Games." He pulls out two note cards and begins to read.

"First, we had a winner one time." He moves on to his second card. "Second, when we died the other seventy-three times, it wasn't always accompanied by crying and pleading."

"Thank you," he concludes. "Now, please give your undivided attention to this message from President Satanman."

A large screen is unfurled at the back of the stage, and the image of a silver-haired man in a neatly tailored black suit appears on it. He glares out at the audience with his piercing red eyes, softly growling.

"Greetings, Slum 12," he begins, with a crooked sneer that exposes a row of razor-sharp steel teeth. "*Extremely evil* greetings. I have one question for you all: Are you ready to die?"

I shudder. For some reason, I can't shake the feeling that there's something...evil about this man. He licks his lips with his forked tongue and continues.

"You'd *better* be ready. For, as we say in the Capitol, 'Garbage men deserve a garbage death, where garbage means painful.'"

With President Satanman done, the Mayor calls up a short, squat woman in a garish pink wig, with a garish living Furbie growing from the side of her head. Her name is Oofie Triptrip, and she is the official agent for Slum 12 sacrifices.

"Greetings, slaves!" she shouts merrily, as she heads over to the old Powerball machine. Inside, there is a Powerball with each of our names on it. The crowd is getting tense, either because they're wondering who will be picked, or because they have a vague feeling that even though lotteries no longer exist, they still have a chance to win.

The machine spits out a pink ball. So, a girl has been chosen first. That must be a good omen—I'm a girl, so the odds of them calling both a girl *and* one named Bratniss must be extremely low.

And I'm right. The name on that pink girl's ball is not Bratniss.

It's Pita Malarkey.

Every single person in the crowd bursts into laughter at the gender-based mix-up, as if it's the funniest thing that's ever happened in Slum 12. Come to think of it, it might be. As you've probably noticed, things are pretty grim around here. People have to devote so much of their time to survival that they don't have much left over to develop senses of humor. I mean, this is Slum 12's most popular joke:

Q. What is black, filled with trash, and men work in it?
A. A mine.

So, yeah. Top Slum 12 woodchip dollar might be shelled out to put spoiled mustard on the dinner table, but ask a Slum 12 local why the chicken crossed the road and he might beat you up for knowing where a chicken is.

But the idea of suggesting that someone is the opposite gender is so earth-shatteringly hilarious to the townspeople that they can't help but laugh and laugh. It's a sound I've heard so few times before in Slum 12. And despite the joy behind it, to me the sound brings a sort of heartache. For this is the laughter of the destitute, the malnourished, and those mysteriously fat people that Third World societies always seem to have. These laughs are pained and shallow, interspersed with high, lonesome yips and barks followed by panting and sniffing, and then back to the bark—*Wait* a second! Get out of here, hyenas! Shoo! *Shoo*!

The hyenas flee down the street. In the Square, their laughter has been replaced with shrill Pita-shrieks. "I'm not a girl!" he cries. "Wait, I mean, don't make me go to the Games!"

But the crowd is having none of it, and has begun chanting at him:

Pita is a girl,
Pita is a girl,
Rah, rah, shish-koom-ba,
Pita is a girl.

But not everyone in Slum 12 is so mean-spirited. Some of them chant something moderately encouraging:

Pita is a girl,
Pita is a girl,
We hope you do well in the tournament, Pita,
But still you are a girl.

One man begins to belt out something a little different…

Party rock is in the house tonight,
Everybody just have a good—BZZZZZT
BZZZZZT BZZZZZT BZZZZZT

…before a line of laser beams quickly cuts him down. The 'Peace'keepers are stridently anti-LMFAO. Of course, they're also anti-laughter. But the politicians would never ban laughter outright, since they enjoy laughing at people who are worse off than they are. After the lasering, the 'Peace'keepers make their way through the crowd, showing anybody who's laughing sad pictures, like of puppies stranded in the rain and that sort of thing. Gradually, there is silence, aside from a group of boys in my class high-fiving each other to celebrate their successful pranking of Pita, and, in the distance, the gentle drizzle of hyenas peeing on our buildings.

Up onstage, Pita looks more helpless and pee-pantsed than ever. The Malarkeys are bakers by trade, not scariness-of-being-selected-for-a-death-tournament-ignorers, and Pita is no exception. In fact, he might be the most unsuitable choice for the Games in Slum 12 history. Ah, wait, what am I talking about? That's always going to be that boy who was born without bones.

But Pita might be a close second. How close? Well, he's so afraid of bees that he won't even spell the word. Instead, he writes it as "b - -", which doesn't solve anything, because as soon as he sees it, he remembers that the letter and the word sound the same, and he starts screaming because, "Ahh! It's a bee shooting its stingers at me!"

Another example: you'll often see him walking around the Crack carrying a seatbelt. No, there aren't any cars in Slum 12. He uses that seatbelt to strap himself into regular seats. Ask him why and he'll solemnly explain that "a chair is unsafe at *any* speed."

So, does that clear things up for you?

As he stares out at the crowd in terror, our eyes meet for a moment. I quickly avert my gaze. Not because I can't stand to see him like this. But, because, well…there's one little thing I forgot to mention about Pita. He's in love with me. Madly, insanely, stalkerishly in love with me. And it's been that way for as long as I can remember.

I think back to the first day of nursery school. When my father dropped me off that morning, I had cried and screamed: I was worried that it might disrupt my plans to hunt one million percent of the time, and, of course, I was correct. Even worse, it was clear that none of my classmates shared my interests. They were way more interested in learning the alphabet or whatever than they were in learning how to rip a moose in half with their bare hands. Then make a helmet out of its skull. Then to use that helmet to help kill more moose. Collect the skull helmets. Combine. Assemble. Super moose skull helmet. Infinite power.

But shortly after I arrived, I saw a dress-up chest in the corner. My spirits rose: I could hurl it through one of the windows and escape! I rushed over. When I picked it up, though, its top flew open, and a boy popped his head up out of the layers of clothing.

"Hi," he said. "I'm Pita."

"Why are you wearing a tiara?" I asked.

"Because when I grow up, I'm going to be the prettiest prince in all the land! And you," he said, hopping out, "Will be my pretty pretty Princess!"

"Nuh-uh," I said, astounded.

"*Yes*-huh," he replied. "Maybe you aren't ready yet. I get it. This is a new situation, you want time to explore it, play with a block or two, eat some Play-Doh. I get it. Go wild. But one day, I'm going to make you mine."

I couldn't believe the audacity of this tiara-wearing three-year-old boy. Who was he to talk to a three-and-a-half-year-old this way?

"You're wrong!" I shouted. "I'm never going to be--"

The next thing I knew, Pita smashed through the very window I had been planning to escape from.

"Aaah!" I could hear him shouting as he ran out deep into the woods, "Bee! Beeeeeeeeeee! BEEEEEEEEEEE! BE-e-E-e-EEE-e-E-eeee!"

Since that day, Pita Malarkey has pursued me relentlessly. He's tried to snare me with gifts, like the time in second grade that he got me a Barbie, which is this kind of prehistoric doll my father would occasionally dig up and give to me to show how fat people used to be.

When gifts failed, he tried to snare me by becoming a sort of platonic best friend, which he hoped would eventually lead to me falling in love with him, after we became close enough for me to see "the real Pita."

"Who are the hot boys? Dish it, sista!" he would say, "Let's rollerblade over to their houses, so you can flirt!"

All of this is bad enough, but recently, there's been a development that's even worse: I think Pita might be getting a bit...stalkery. I can't be sure, but there was an incident a few months ago that got me thinking. Thinking that maybe, Pita was trying another route to my heart. One through my father.

Or rather, by replacing my father. Because one afternoon, the doorbell rang, and there on our doorstep sat a massive loaf of bread in the shape of a human, with a big nametag that read "Loaf Erickson." My mom looked the crusty Nordic breadfellow over and screamed with joy, "I am instantly in love with you!

Like any stepfather made entirely of bread, Loaf had some curious habits. He would lie completely still for incredibly long periods of time and, each week without fail, he would grow what I had to swear was a full-body mold beard. But that didn't matter. He was warm, soft, and smelled of butter. My mother swooned. Meanwhile, I noticed that one of Loaf's eyes was a video camera.

I also noticed that inside Loaf's stomach was a sound recorder, that one of his feet had a vacuum in it that collected hair, and that higher up, in the calf, was a hair-doll maker. Loaf's right eye had what appeared to be an infrared camera. For a supposedly normal bread-stepdad, he had a lot of stalking gadgetry baked inside him. In other words, Loaf Erickson *stunk* of Pita.

I sent Loaf to bread hell on a stormy night. "What are you doing?!" shouted my mother when she walked into the kitchen to find me assembling knives, cups of water and other bread-unfriendly weapons. But before I could explain that this was a routine surgery and that no, no, nothing to see here, move along please, ignore any yeasty screams, she had brandished a blade from her mom cane, and told me that whatever I did unto Loaf would befall me, except tenfold.

"Why are you suddenly speaking in biblical terms, mo—"

"Layeth thou one fingereth on my Loaf, and thou shalt die, daughter of thine."

"Mine. You mean *mine*."

"Whatever. Also no allowance for one *week*."

"Mom, you've never given me an allowance."

"I'll kill you!"

So it came down to a simple choice: kill Loaf and be killed by mom, or let Pita spy on me. The choice was simple.

It's incredible how easily a wet knife slides through a bread-man's neck. I'll never forget the sound of my mother's hatchet scraping against the walls as she methodically pursued me that night. "Bratniss, Bratniss, come meet your new daddy. He's long and hatchet-y, and he can't wait to meet you," she sang out.

I'm pulled back to the present by Pita's shrieks. "No! I am *not* a girl!" he wails through his shirt, which he has stretched over his head in an attempt to hide his tears. He's crying so hard now that he's getting that fat kid in a white t-shirt at a pool look. "How can this be happening to me? Mr. Bear, *what are we going to do*?" He glances down at his side, and his face turns white. "Oh my God. Mr. Bear, where are you? Are you hiding behind my bed again? This is no time for your silly bear games! I need you right now!"

We're all victims, here: Pita, the crowd, and, most importantly, me. Every cell of my body is crying out for me to end this. It's just too mortifying.

Wait, wait, wait. Come on. I can deal with thirty seconds of seeing someone embarrass themselves. I don't even need to look! I'll just stare at the ground, and ride this out. And, already, I can feel it beginning to pass!

And now that I've successfully overcome it, I can look up again! I do, and Pita's halfway naked.

"Remember what they say, Pita," he says under his breath, "If you get nervous onstage, imagine that the entire crowd...sees you naked. That's it, right?" He begins unzipping his jeans. "Right?"

Well, that's it for me. "I'LL DO IT!" I shout, "I'LL TAKE HIS PLACE!"

A deep silence falls over the crowd. Ah, crud. I did it. I went and volunteered for a death tournament. I see Oofie's bedazzled finger pointing at me. Her voice booms demonically.

"YOU!"

She takes a nip from her helium flask and her voice returns to normal.

"*You*...are a girl?" she repeats, as Pita nervously twirls one of his braids.

"Uh, yeah, technically, but maybe we can look past that, and—"

"And you wish to TAKE HIS PLACE AT THE—OH DAMNIT, HOLD ON."

She takes a long, hard slug from the bottle, really choking that helium down. Tears stream from her face as the sludge slides down her throat. She polishes off the entire thing and sloppily wipes her mouth in that way that people with problems do. "Okay, that should hold me until dusk," she says. "So, you want to take his place? That is so brave of you, darling. Especially because we were actually going to just pick another name."

"Oh, great! Let's do that, and forget about this whole—"

"But this makes everything so much easier. Who has time to pick a single ball from a Powerball machine these days? Get onstage."

I realize then what a catastrophic mistake I've made. But perhaps there is still a way to escape...

"Sounds good, Oofie," I say, with a big smile. "But do you mind if I give my sister Pig a hug?"

She beams at me. "Not at all, sweetheart."

I rush over to Pig and embrace her tightly.

"*Listen,*" I whisper in her ear, "*They just called your name. Go on up there, be strong for me. No tears, now.*"

"Uh...Bratniss? You're mic'd up, hon," Oofie calls out from the stage.

"Ha ha! Of course, of course," I reply, "Just a little joke between sisters, you know how it is! Now, I'll simply start walking up to the stage. Here I am, getting closer. Closer still!" But my trick of sprinting directly out of the Square fools no one, and I am dragged onto the stage. My God, this is actually happening. I'm going to die.

Then it hits me. Death isn't even the worst part of this. Oh, no, not by a long shot. Because I just saved Pita: *he must think I like him now.* And if I don't live to survive the Games and tell him otherwise, he'll go to his grave thinking it, and so will everyone else.

But before I can find a different boy and make him my boyfriend, Oofie grabs my hand, and places a small, plastic-wrapped item in it. When I look closer, my heart begins to race. *Candy.*

This is only the second piece of candy I've had in my life, after that hunk of rat meat that fell in the sugar jar once. All thoughts of death and Pita-liking slip away for the moment as I gaze at it, imagining what it would feel like on my tongue, and my second and third tongues, which humans eventually got from using cell phones too much. Then, as quickly as it was given, the candy is taken away.

"It's a ritual," Oofie explains, casually pocketing the shit-flavored lollipop. "Sorry, kid." Then she jumps right back into the Reaming, directing her anger at the schoolboys who pranked Pita.

"All right, you little twerps, I hope you know what karma is, because it's right about to bite you on your butts. There's a higher power, who makes sure we all get what we deserve, not factoring in kids with cancer and all those people who die unhappy. Mark my words..."

Looking at the schoolboys of Slum 12, I can't help but feel a bit of comfort. Their work in the mines has made them strong and brave, and having one of them as something of a partner in the Games wouldn't be too bad. I'd even be happy with a kid from the one place here that's worse than the Crack: a quaint underground township known as the Taint, which is the spot where Slum 12's sewage and corpse streams converge. I bet those Taint kids would love a chance to get their sludgy paws on some surface-dwellers. And you never know, maybe I'll even get that one boy standing at the corner of the stage: the incredibly handsome, incredibly honorable Peeta Mellark.

"And with that *lesson* in mind," continues Oofie, glaring, "the Slum 12 male sacrifice for this year's Hunger But Mainly Death Games is..."

Oofie reads the Powerball.

"Damnit. Pita Malarkey."

The roar of the crowd almost drowns out Pita's wails. Almost. But nobody takes notice, because they're all too busy celebrating the fact that they haven't been chosen this year, by performing the Slum 12 Slide, a traditional dance with urban undertones. A DJ's voice booms out over the loudspeakers:

Two steps to the right!
Two steps to the lef'!
Now stand up straight, cuz you's not dead!

As the crowd dances on, Oofie gravely electric slides over toward us. "It's time to meet your mentor, kiddos," she says, artfully pulling jazz fingers across her face.

She then Crip-walks over to the end of the stage, where she beckons to a big, bedraggled, be-bearded bear of a man who, despite the five foot high stage upon which Oofie stands, still towers over her. Over the clamor of the crowd, I can hear only snippets of what Oofie is yelling at the man. From what I can make out, it's...*a harsh warning about copyright laws*?

Finally, the giant man steps on stage with her and dougies over to us. When he speaks, it's in a booming brogue, "Pleased ter meetcha! Hagridmitch be the name. An' you must be th' newest students o' Hogwar—"

SLAP! Oofie's hand leaves a bright red mark on Hagridmitch's face.

"What did I *tell* you? You'll get us all canned! His name is *Pita*. And her name is *Ratface*."

"It's Bratniss," I say.

"Ratlips?"

"Bratniss."

"Catpiss?"

"Fine," I sigh. "Catpiss."

"No, no, I'll meet you halfway," she replies. "Stacey it is."

"Looks more like a Hermione ter me, but—" Hagridmitch interjects. But before he can finish, Oofie pulls a collapsible spiked bat out of her purse, and begins whacking him with it.

"Bad Hagridmitch! Bad, bad Hagridmitch! What did I tell you about copyright laws? Do you want to get *sued*? Is that what you want?"

Slowly, remorsefully, Hagridmitch gets to his feet. "Aw, I'm sorry, Oofie. I am, I tell ye. But I've got jes' the thing ter make it up ter you's kids," he says, reaching into his bag.

"Hagridmitch, you shouldn't have," Oofie responds.

"Now, now, it ain't nothin'!" he says with a wide grin.

"No, I mean you shouldn't have by law," says Oofie. "Even *giving gifts* is illegal here!" We all crack a smile, because *wow we live in a cruddy place.*

"Slum 12 laws be darned," Hagridmitch says, pushing Oofie to the side and opening his satchel to reveal...a basket of fresh eggs.

The eggs give us all pause. Even Oofie is taken aback by the gesture. In Slum 12, you see, eggs cost more than human life (which is, of course, incredibly cheap here, but you get the point). As you know, an egg comes from a chicken. And we all know where that chicken comes from. Yes, that's right, the Chicken Overlord, a hermit who lives deep in the forest and is a *notorious* jerk when it comes to bartering. We're talking your wife for an eggshell; that brand of jerk.

"Thank you, Hagridmitch," I say. "They look delicious."

"*Delicious*?" he sputters. "Why, I never hard a such a thing! These be none o' yer normal *eatin'* eggs, child" he responds, looking into the TV cameras and cocking an eyebrow, "These be *dragon* eggs."

Oofie's hands curl into fists and she barks, "Get him out of here! You're *done*! *Canned*!"

Meanwhile, Hagridmitch squats down so that he's eye level with us and asks, "Do ye want to meet my pet giant-spider? His name is—" Oofie tackles Hagridmitch.

As we are being led away from the rather one-sided brawl, Magma, the mayor's daughter brushes by me. And as she does, I'm pinned to the floor by something she discretely tosses at me. I push it off of me to find that it's an enormous gold pin of a huge, flightless bird with a stupendously idiotic smile on its face—a mockstrich, the creature the Capitol once tried to turn genetically engineer into a war-machine to help put an end to the rebellion. The plan fizzled after it became clear that the birds preferred laughing at people and collecting shiny pipe-cleaners more than killing rebels.

"Magma!" I yell after her. "Why did you give me this? Is it a present?"

She whips around, eyes wide with horror. "*Don't say the p-word*!" she whispers desperately. But it's too late.

"Who here engaged in present-distribution?" shouts the leader of the 'Peace'keepers present task-force that's zoomed down from a helicopter to surround us.

"Nobody!" I manage. "This isn't a present. It's my grandmother's lucky mockstrich pin. I was just saying how much I wish my grandmother were *present* today."

"Why the heck would you wish that?" the leader asks. "This would be a terrible moment for her."

"Look, are you going to laser me or not?" I ask.

The leader eyes us suspiciously, and then turns to walk away. "I guess today's your lucky day, apart from the Hunger But Mainly Death Games thing," he says.

But I avoid that trap only to fall straight into another. Because when I turn around, I see something that fills me with terror.

No. No, no, no, no, no. This can't be happening.

Pita is on one knee, looking in my direction.

And he is asking me something.

"Will you marry me?"

Pita sweeps past me and grasps the hands of his best friend: Will Umarimi.

Phew, that was close. But I'll have to be more careful going forward. Pandumb is a nation in which improbable twists occur with terrifying frequency, and if you're not vigilant you can end up dead, after which M. Night Shyamalan might use you in whatever his latest abysmally bad movie is.

Pita bends down to speak with his friend. Will Umarimi is a small person. No, not a "*midget.*" Or a "*dwarf.*" Those are hateful terms, And shame on you for thinking them. Will is a dwidget, which is a super-helpful, non-offensive term if you don't want to sit there and guess which kind of short person you're looking at. I should probably mention here that no one has ever had the heart to inform Will that he's a dwidget.

"I'm telling you," Will says to Pita, "you need to hide as much as you can in the arena. Holes in trees, cupboards. Backpacks will do, too."

"I can't, I'm..." Pita's voice drifts off.

"You're what? Why can't you just hide in small places? If it works for me, it'll work for you. We're best friends, remember?"

"Okay, fine," says Pita. "I'll hide in small places. Anything else?"

"I guess just that if you want to stay alive, you have to be ready to do what it takes."

Pita nods solemnly in understanding. So, he realizes that he'll have to drop his pursuit of me. I'm a bit relieved to know that on top of everything else, I won't have to grapple with any teen love issues in the arena.

"And what it takes," Will continues, "Is the power of love! If you love something, never let it go! Totally latch onto it and turn it into your kissing post! Only then can you win the Hunger But Mainly Death Games!"

Pita nods his head in vigorous, celebratory understanding, all while maintaining unblinking, drooling eye contact with me, and howling in that wolfy way cartoon characters in love do. Then Pita gently punts Will back into the crowd. He soars gracefully through the air, too high for me to grab and strangle.

But I have to remind myself that some of my anger is misplaced. After all, it's not Will's fault that I'm about to be shuttled off to the Games with a guy who has an insane crush on me. No, the real villains here are the people who enforce Pandumb's evil policies. The people who, out of their wild lust for kid death-based basic programming, host a nationwide, televised event in which teenagers are forced to kill each other in a dynamic, action-packed arena, with lots of cool, futuristic weapons and amazing traps, and…

And the more I think about it, the more amazing this all sounds on the spectators' end. I guess the only thing I can actually get angry about is that my own best friend hasn't come to say goodbye to me, and maybe to smack some sense into Pita, too. Where can he be? Where can Kobayashi the talking dog be?

Oh, wait, I mean, "Greta." Perhaps he's too busy with his experiments. After all, Mondays are when he tapes pencils to his canines and puts on his walrus simulator hat.

But these are my final moments in Slum 12. I'd have hoped I'd be able to share them with someone I cared for. So I guess there's just you, diary, or whatever it is that I'm writing in/talking into. I suppose that you will have to provide the comfort I would have received from—AGH! An arm is thrust around my neck in a headlock from behind, and I'm slammed into the ground.

"Cross-face chicken wing," Greta hisses into my ear, tightening his grip. "Go ahead, try to escape."

But I can't. Greta's forearm is jammed against my throat and, nice as escaping sounds, lack of oxygen has always weakened my body for some reason.

"Now, quick, stand up so I can show you how to take a punch in the face."

With what little air I have left I manage to squeak out a few words, "Greta, let go! I just want to say goodbye to you."

And then, as quickly as he was on me, Greta releases the hold.

"Sorry, Bratniss. No time for that. Only time for chokeholds. I've got to get back to the fort immediately. I'm making a…" Greta glances around furtively and cuts his voice down to a whisper, "…b-o-a-m-b."

So, that's what he's been doing all along! Building a boamb! I should have known that Greta would stop at nothing to save me, regardless of his terrible spelling! Still, I can't believe how daring his plan is—to bomb the Hunger But Mainly Death Games arena!

"That's right," he says, "Blowing up the Blob is the only way to make it rain free sandwiches."

"Oh."

"Here," he says, handing me a slip of paper, "take this poem with you. I've really gotta get back,"

I look at the paper. It's not a poem.

"Greta, this is just a page torn out of your diary! It says here that if there's one girl at school who you want to run your experiments on, it's—"

"Wrong poem!" he says, snatching the paper out of my hand. He replaces it with a new paper, before slinking as mysteriously as he can back into the crowd. I put the shard of beer bottle glass I use as a monocle in front of my eye and read:

There was once a Sweet Princess
SCHFFPPLLLTTT
Wait a second where is her head
Hand me those pliers, Intern Larry
These wires are all on wrong you fool
ZZT ZZT ZZT
All systems are go
Robot princess up and running
But we are not done here
Readjust those ear-pegs, Larry

Thank you, Larry
Okay now we are done

Charming guy, that Greta. Helpful, too. Just then, a 'Peace'keeper grabs me by the arm and begins leading me and Pita to the outskirts of town, where we'll be held until our transport to the Capitol arrives. For the first time, it hits me: they're actually going to make me do this. My mind races—what was it that my grandfather told me when I was little, as I sat upon his knee? What was that advice he had about accidentally volunteering for a death tournament? Oh, yeah: "Do not ever do that, Bratniss. Not in a million years." Crap.

But when we arrive at my new quarters, I can't help but remember grandpa was kind of an idiot, because this is the nicest cage I've ever seen! Shiny metal bars on all sides and wheels on the underside bars for easy transporting. So, the housewidow tales were true: the Capitol really does know how to treat a prisoner. "You go to the bathroom through the bars on the floor," the guard says sweetly.

But the wonders don't end there: the town mule drags the cage up to the administrative building, where the cage is picked up and tossed inside the most beautiful room I have ever seen in my life. It has all the comforts of home—no couch, no rug, and huge, human-hating bats on the ceiling, right down to the black mold that covers basically everything. But the Capitol hasn't stopped there—no, not at all. They've gone so far as to install a table! And not just an ordinary table. Ordinary tables are bare and broken and on fire. This table has four entire legs, and a bowl filled to the brim with a slice of bread.

I'm inspecting the slice for rats when my mother and Pigrose show up. I quickly pocket it, knowing that if mom sees sliced bread she'll have a full-on Loaf flashback and probably try to kill me.

"What bread, you old loon?" I accidentally blurt out.

"How could you leave us!?" my mom yells at me through the bars. For a second, I think about trying to explain that the Reaming is a lottery and that it wasn't my *choice* to—oh wait, it was totally my choice. I *volunteered* to go to the Hunger But Mainly Death Games. Damnit. Mom kind of has me there.

"You're out of this family now," she spits, desperately trying to wiggle her head through the bars so she can get a clean bite at me. "No more Sunday family trips to rat church, no more waking up each morning to the friendly neighborhood doo-doo man Luigi, calmly screaming to let him inside before the street-badgers eat him! And need I remind you, you're leaving it all for a lousy death tournament!"

My mom may hook up with bread, but she has a point. And for the first time, I start to feel terribly sad about leaving these two behind. My mother must realize it, because she pockets her knife and opens her arms. But when I go in for a hug, I lean too far forward, and the slice of bread falls out. Oh shi—

"WHAT is my husband's severed hand doing on the floor!?" she shouts, shaking the bars of my cage. "MURDERER! You *murderer*!"

The 'Peace'keepers come to grab her, but she's too strong for them, and bursts free. Fortunately, their highly trained anti-mom gorilla is stronger. "I want my husband back, you bread-racists!" she shrieks through Koko's thick fur, as he carries her out.

I'm left alone with Pigrose. Here, in the few moments I have left with precious little Pig, I need to sum up all my older sisterly knowledge into a few parting words. As I gaze at her, she still seems so small, so vulnerable. But she was right this morning. She's not a baby anymore. And now, she'll have to fend for herself entirely. All I can do to help is speak from the heart.

I grab her by the cheeks, force her face between the bars and say to her, "Cow says 'moo,' Pig. 'Moooo.'"

Pita's cage has been set down next to mine, and he's saying goodbye to his parents, Clark Malarkey and #0432, a mom-bot.

"Watch out for bugs, kiddo!" says Clark, slapping a can of bug spray into Pita's palm. "And, remember that old saying: 'if it's leaves of three, that's just for wiping pee.' Or maybe it's 'when leaves is four, yo' butt's gon' be sore…'"

Clark pauses, deep in thought, before saying, "You know what, to be safe maybe just wipe your butt with rocks."

"HELLO PITA," says #0432, clamping her metal pincers onto Pita's shoulder. "I AM YOUR MOTHER. BIRTHING AND BREASTFEEDING EQUIPPED. ENJOY CONSUMPTION OF GRAHAM CRACKER, CHOC-O-LATE AND MARSHMALLOW DESSERT SANDWICHES WITH THE OTHER HU-MANS."

"Wait," says Pita. "You guys realize this isn't camp I'm going to, right?"

"Here, son," says Pita's dad, handing him a plastic bag through the bars of the cage, "I brought some swim trunks and your sun tan lotion. But you know how sensitive your skin is, so don't push it. If you think you're getting a burn, stay indoors at all times. The counselors will understand, and the other boys will respect you."

The Malarkeys are ushered out and Pita and I are left alone. "Whew!" Pita exclaims as the door slams shut, "I thought those totally lame bozos would never leave us alone!"

Oh my God. It's already begun. Does anybody know if there's some way to turn off your hearing? Like, I don't know, a secret button you can press on your head, or some kind of meditation?

Pita's tone softens. "I...look, I know I'm a real idiot sometimes, so I'll shut up now. But I need to tell you something: I appreciate what you did out there today, all right? And I'm sorry. I'm sorry that our first day of going out has to be this way."

"Pita, listen to me: that was not—"

"Shh, shh," he says. "You don't have to hide it. Neither of us has to, anymore. We're in love."

"No, we are not!"

"Say what you want, Bratniss, but your actions have spoken louder than a trillion words. And I want mine to do the same: so I'm giving up my former ways. I know you see me as a dangerous man, something of a playboy. But I'm ready to leave all of that behind for you. I'm sorry you had to do something so drastic to get me to realize that."

Before I can answer or vomit, the doors are flung open and we're carried out to the train that will take us to the Capitol. A small crowd has formed to watch us go, and there, at the front, struggling to break through a line of 'Peace'keepers.

"Bratniss!" he calls, "Bratniss!" But he can't get through. Before the doors of the train slide shut, I can hear his final message to me. "Always remember, it doesn't matter if you die, because this is all probably just the dream of some dinosaur, anyway!

The moment I step inside, I have to cover my eyes from the unbearable brightness. As it turns out, Capitol folks live by the light of stuff other than fire. The Capitol lights its rooms with tiny glass beads filled with distilled light-juice, which are powered by a colony of inch-long bunnies that live in the walls. At least that's what Oofie tells me. I don't have a clue why she's laughing so hard, but I can't think of a better explanation.

I am taken to my room, which is actually just a larger cage for my cage to be locked into. It's filled with the strangest objects, and Oofie can tell I'm confused.

"Do you know what any of this is?" she coos.

"Not exactly."

She points to a stack of big, cushiony chairs and says, "Let's start simple. Massage chairs. With a special massage chair massage chair on the bottom to massage the massage chairs. Keeps 'em happy and healthy. Makes sense now, right?"

Kind of. Well, not really. Why would they need multiple massage chairs? And what the heck is a massa—

"Cat got your mouthsnake?" Oofie says, handing me a tin can. "Let's start even simpler. Look. A watch in a can. Now, you see the genius of it all."

"But why do you need these things?" I ask.

"Why does anyone need anything?" Oofie replies breezily. "You own things so you can have them. Then you don't need them anymore."

She has me there, I guess. Wait, no she doesn—

"Let's level with each other, Brat," Oofie says. "We both want the same thing here: Dumbbuxx®. I'm your agent, and I get you sponsors. Sponsors get you and me money. And Dumbbuxx® buys us stuff like hovercars and pocketdogs."

"No! What I want is to not die in the arena!" I pause. "And maybe a pocketdog or two if I survive," I add.

"You're not listening, beb. Think of it this way. Some rich benefactor sees you in the arena and takes a shining to you. He likes your moves. He digs your style. 'Hey,' he thinks to himself, 'I'm going to spend one billion dollars to get that little missy a toothbrush.'"

"But I brought my own toothbrush," I say. "And, anyway, a toothbrush isn't going to help me win the Hunger But Mainly Death Games."

Oofie's eyes narrow. "That attitude is gonna get you killed. And even worse, prevent me from getting my bonus. So when I say jump, you jump. And when I tell you that *Dr. Doolittle 7: Rise of the Planet of the Hermit Crabs* is a good idea, you throw on your animal doctor lab coat, and goddamnit, you learn how to talk to hermit crabs. So you'd better listen to me when I say you need sponsors to survive. Now why don't us girls do some window shopping?" she says with a conspiratorial air, handing me a catalog.

On its cover is an illustration of a man in a mirror tuxedo throwing a lavish party on the roof-deck of his hot air balloon yacht. Far below, you can see innocent children struggling to survive in the Hunger But Mainly Death Games. Disgusted, I flip past the cover and open to a random page:

"Two pine needles," it reads. "Who KNOWS what a resourceful sacrifice could do with these rascals! Just thinking about it fills us with wonder and amazement. $20 billion."

I flip to the next page.

"Water! The most vital substance on Earth (at least for those poors outside the Capitol who don't hydrate using Water 2: Sprite®). Any sacrifice who doesn't have it is sure to die. So send them some of this thirst-quenching liquid and watch them rise to the top! You can also just buy it and throw it out, so that the sacrifice will be more likely to die of thirst. Either way, you will get a tax deduction. $1 trillion per bubble wrap bubble-worth of water (bubbles may include large portions of air)."

I keep flipping, trying to find something, *anything*, that could be useful to me. One 'gently-used' earplug? The dust from a moth that flew into a windshield? Suddenly, I realize something:

"Oofie, these all suck."

"I can't help you if you won't help yourself, Bratniss!" she says briskly.

"You don't need to help me. I don't want any of this. Bye," I say, as I dramatically turn and walk into the bars of my cage.

Later that evening, I'm let out and escorted down to the dining room. After I've been given my rabies vaccine, and the standard "You start foaming at the mouth at the table then we put you *down*, girlie" talk, we're seated. Our group consists of me, Pita, Oofie, Hagridmitch, several of the technicians who tend to our cages, and a few Xeroxes. Xeroxes are the poor souls who have been sentenced to a life of servitude in the Capitol for committing some trivial crime back in the Slums.

According to the company handbook, they're referred to as "personal assistants," but if you ask me, they're little more than slaves.

The Xeroxes are famed for their encyclopedic knowledge, which they obtain in arduous training sessions. Of course, Oofie is as eager to show off her possession's skills as if they were her own.

"You two simply must see what the Capitol has been kind enough to train these Xeroxes to do. Siri? Which one of you is Siri? Present yourself!" A young Xerox with flowing blond hair steps forward and curtsies.

"Good evening, Miss Triptrip. How may I serve you?" she asks softly, her hands clasped together and her eyes turned towards the floor.

Oofie pokes me. "These freaks know the answer to everything, darling. Go ahead, try her out."

"Hmm..." I say, trying to think of something that won't insult the intelligence of this bright-eyed girl. "Okay. Siri, what is the meaning of life?"

She responds with a demure smile. "All evidence to date suggests that it's successfully avoiding suicide."

"Ahh-ha-ha, charming, simply charming!" says Oofie. "Who knew that they would have taught you to be so deliciously funny! Well, off to the gallows, Siri. That's your punishment for failure."

"No! Wait!" I protest. But she's already gone, and dinner is being served. Life, it would appear, is cheap to the Capitol. Or maybe that was already clear from everything else.

When the first course is placed in front of me, I can hardly believe my eyes: the meat that they're serving looks nothing at all like roadkill. But, weirdly, this doesn't appear to be meat at all. It's a plate of pale green mush with some brown mush on the side.

"Oofie, what is this?"

She rolls her eyes. "It's organic, grass fed, redehydrated Alsatian snow peas with kale sausage. It'll help you cut some unwanted fat off those bones. Wouldn't want you to die of fat cancer before you started the games."

Unwanted fat? Last time I checked, in Slum 12, 4'3" and 64 pounds is perfectly normal. I distinctly remember the girls at school being amazed at how much I could eat on Thursday pizza box lunches. "Eat the cardboard, rat-girl! Eat the cardboard!" they'd chant, cheering me on like the good friends they were.

Oofie continues explaining the menu. On the train, our food will be "gluten-free vegan," and is "macrobiotic, probiotic, antibiotic and neurobiotic..."

I decide against using my spork and tentatively stick my spoonfe into the mush, which causes a yellowish ooze to spill out. Everything smells like mulch.

"There aren't any other options on the menu, are there?" I ask with a grimace. To my surprise, the people around me erupt in pained cries.

"This must be some sick ploy!" shouts one of the cage technicians. "What if she's trying to give us cancer? Oh my God, I think that just hearing what she said gave my ears cancer. I THINK I HAVE EAR CANCER!"

Even Oofie looks terrified. "Take it back! Take it back!" she pleads. "You may have nothing to live for, but there's no reason to sentence us to cancer-death! And eating algae we scraped off the seafloor is clearly the only way to avoid that!"

"Sheesh! All right!" I exclaim. "I take it back!" These people may be crazy, but Pita has to know what I'm talking about!

But he doesn't. Or at least that's how he acts. I guess the last thing I should expect from the boy who is madly in love with me is for him to stick up for me at a dinner. How totally unreasonable of me. Instead he just kind of sits there, in his chair, like an empty, empty chair—wait. Pita isn't in his chair.

That's when I realize that there's no way the table leg could have been painting my toenails and blowing on them underneath the table this entire time. I lift up the table cover and sure enough, there he is, bottle of polish in hand, and...well, my nails look really good. One toenail is a little smudged from what appears to be drool but I'd happily give take that in exchange for—No! What am I thinking?! "Get away, Pita!"

He scurries up from under the table.

"You know what they say, Bratniss," he tells me with a grin. "'If a man can't handle giving the woman of his dreams an expert mani-pedi, he doesn't deserve getting lots of kisses from her at the end of their romantic first date!'"

"This isn't a date!"

"Then why has everybody left us alone?" I look around, and he's right. The room is empty. Then the door slides open and a man in a Hazmat suit steps in.

"Sorry to break up the date, you two. But this room has been declared a potential Cancer Zone. Something to do with someone speaking negatively about our dining staff's delicious offerings. I know, I know, it all sounds a bit far-fetched, but to be on the safe side, you're going to have to vacate immediately."

I rush out, desperate to avoid further "date" time with Pita. It's not only annoying, it's also such an insane way to waste time. With the tournament rapidly approaching, I need to stop thinking about anything except how to survive. I need someone who can put things into perspective for me; someone who knows the Hunger But Mainly Death Games, but won't be insane. If possible, even, someone who won't be drunk and babble on about wizards and magic. With that in mind, I stupidly seek out Hagridmitch.

I find him on the floor of the train's wine cellar, where all the moonshine is kept. But I can't get him to wake up. I look around the cellar for something that might rouse him. Hey, over there's a bucket that says "hydrochloric acid" on it. Whatever that stuff is I'm sure it will do the trick. But then I notice the pail of water in the far corner. That could definitely work, too.

But that's the far corner. Way too far to walk. Let's try this acid stuff. I'm midway through tipping the bucket over when Hagridmitch shoots up off the ground—"Deatheaters! Look out, child!" he says as he scoops me up in his massive arms and dives behind a cardboard box.

"Hagridmitch, what are you—"

A finger the size of my head mashes against my face. "Shhhh..." he says, nervously glancing over the box.

Hagridmitch finally begins to trust the silence of the wine cellar and calms down. I figure it's finally time to get some answers. "Hagridmitch, can you tell me—"

"O' course," he says, and instantly launches into a long explanation of this super weird story. Now, I honestly have no idea what Hagridmitch is talking about, nor do I get what Oofie is so worried about him getting us in trouble for, so I won't ruin any part of his story, except to provide you with a few details for some general background: Dumbledore dies in the next-to-last book, Snape is a double agent for the good guys, and Voldemort's soul is in seven different objects that Harry destroys."

I'm not going to lie. His story is really crazy. But, as he's finishing up, I start to get the impression that he's at least telling the truth. "...and then ol' Hagridmitch finally had his way with Hermione. And we're not talkin' one 'n done here," he says, raising his eyebrows.

"Hagridmitch, listen to me for a second. I need to talk to you."

And finally, he stops and listens to me. So I ask him about the Games, and how to survive, and why the title of the games is about food when the games are really just about killing each other, and several other in-Games girl-hygiene related questions I won't share here (but will post on the book's official website: www.hungergamesparody.com).

Hagridmitch considers me sadly for a moment, before bowing his head. "I can't help ye," he says.

"But *why*? Why can't you help me?!"

"I'm terribly sorry. But thar's a very good reason 'ndeed."

But I think he knows that I deserve an answer. Hagridmitch looks around the cellar, making sure no one is there to hear, before he leans in and whispers into my ear...

"The reason I can't tell ye...is that I'm pooping me pants right now."

"Quit playing around, Hagridmitch," I say. But, boy oh boy, I realize pretty quickly that this man ain't playin', as I reluctantly become a member of the "I've Seen Someone's Pants Inflate Like a Balloon Club." The force of it has caused Hagridmitch to pass out, so I survey the scene in silence. It's grim, all right. This isn't even the kind of situation where it'd be best to throw the underwear out. I think the only option here might be to throw Hagridmitch himself out.

Pita pops his head out of a nearby vase.

"All this hubbub has awoken the Pita-snake from his snake-charming basket!" he says, rolling his shoulders all around and waving his arms up and down.

"Pita, what the hell are you doing in there?" I ask, even though I already know the answer. "And did you really think those binoculars would work from inside a sealed ceramic container?"

"Sss!" he says. "You must leave immediately! The venom of the Pita-snake is dangerous; very dangerous indeed! One ounce could fill you with endless love for the first boy you lay eyes on." He wiggles his neck and moves towards me with puckered lips. "Now, let's spice things up a little," he says. "Put this on."

"No! I am not putting on a neon green leather snake costume! How did you even get it?"

"That's not important. The only thing that matters is to not put it on all that convincingly, because I'm really scared of snakes. Maybe put a t-shirt on over it? Or wear one of those hats that looks like a baby rabbit."

"I'll *consider* putting it on if you take care of this mess."

"Deal! Deal deal deal!"

"Deal," I agree, throwing the costume in the trash and running up the stairs two at a time. But as I shut the door behind me, another thought comes into my mind. What if Pita is doing this as part of some cunning ploy to win the Hunger But Mainly Death Games? Getting our mentor on his side, to help ensure that he is the last kid standing?

It's tough to say. On the one hand, I sometimes have a hard time understanding the intentions of others. I wonder if I might even be a tiny bit autistic. But then the train hits a bump, and I brush any thought of that aside as a box of toothpicks falls and spills its contents across the floor.

"Two-hundred-seventeen," I say.

Anyway, there's a much more likely explanation for Pita's behavior: he's trying to guilt me into liking him. If you've ever been the object of a sort of nerdy guy's love, you know the drill. My guess is that it's, quite literally, the oldest trick in the book. Like, way long ago, a group of young cavemen got together to attempt to solve their biggest problem: lack of girlfriends. They didn't have girlfriends for a number of reasons: they were no good at hunting; they couldn't perform any daring feats of strength and bravery; they were so allergic to pollen, and dust, and bright light, that they had to spend most of their time in-cave. And don't get me started on their little peach-fuzz mustaches that they were too clueless about to get rid of.

Anyway, these caveboys came up with a plan to overcome all that: they would become personal martyrs for the cavegirl they liked, in the hopes that, eventually, she would have no choice but to return their love. Some would do it by always letting the girl copy off of their cavekid homework. Others would do it by becoming a sort of sisterly friend—gossiping with their crushes about other girls in the cavegrade, talking about caveoutfits, even sometimes going so far as to help set up their crushes with a cavejock, in the hopes that he would be sorta douchey to her, and that after about their fifth breakup, the crush would realize that her true love had been there all along, and that his obsession with playing games on his caveTI-83 graphing calculator was actually extremely cool.

Of course, it's never worked, even once. But that hasn't stopped the boys from trying. It shouldn't be a problem, right? Having some boy head-over-heels in sorrowful love with you should be, at worst, an ego boost; and at best, the closest you'll ever be to getting that trick-performing, talking monkey pet you've always dreamed of.

Unfortunately, it's never that simple. Because the guys who do stuff like that actually want you to be a talking monkey pet of their own, whose "trick" is being all relationship-y with them.

All of this is especially true of Pita. Case-in-point: one year, he gave me a valentine with a drawing of a frail elderly couple on the front and a message inside that read, "My idea of a perfect relationship is an old man gently tending to his wife as she slips into Alzheimer's."

"I hope I can care for you like that one day," he had written below.

But if Pita thinks any of it's going to sway me, he's mistaken. I don't owe him a thing. When I reach the hallway of the train, I'm surprised to find that, once again, there isn't a soul in sight. Not my cage technician, not my head-cage technician, not my leg-cages technician, not even the child from the Capitol whom they have follow me around and do stuff like play hopscotch everywhere in order to remind me how crappy my situation is. I soon find out why: "ATTACK IMMINENT! ATTACK IMMINENT!" booms a voice over a loudspeaker. The sliding doors at the end of the corridor fly open.

"Take this!" Oofie shouts, tossing me a ray gun. She flips a nearby table on its side and pulls me behind. "They're coming!"

"*Who's* coming?" I ask.

At that moment, we hear the screeching sound of the metal door being torn off. A horrifying, reptilian creature bursts in.

"GROK!!!" it roars. No time to think. I blast it straight in the head, which explodes in a cloud of green blood. Oofie and I slump back against the table.

"That thing, it was an alien, wasn't it?" I ask, breathlessly. "Aliens attacked, didn't they? Humanity is going to have to band together to defeat the alien horde! Forget about things like the Games, we need to band together!"

"What? That was just another sacrifice. Her body had a bad reaction to the tracking device implantation."

I'm speechless. So, that thing was my first victim of the Hunger But Mainly Death Games. It's an odd feeling. I'm lucky that the situation fits the rules I've secretly laid out for myself: only kill another Sacrifice if they're clearly very evil and trying their hardest to murder you.

That's when I notice the creature is holding two neatly wrapped presents. Addressed to me and Oofie.

"Uh, Oofie?" I ask. "That thing was definitely trying to hurt us...right?"

"Oh man, look at the time. Gotta jet," says Oofie, breezing out of the room. A moment later, she comes back in and gently lifts the ray gun out of my hands. "Thanks, doll."

The door then bursts open and Pita enters, dragging Hagridmitch behind him. Pita's wrapped him up in a huge tarp.

"I tried my best," he pants. "He's just so damn big, almost like he's a giant's half-brother!"

From inside the bag, Hagridmitch hollers, "Th' Order of th' Phoenix isn't going ter like this, of that ye can be certain! They're gonna hang ye, just like they hanged old Mrs. Weasley fer poisonin' Fred an' George when she got sick o' their tricks! They will, I tell ye!" He struggles vainly to get free.

Oofie peeks her head in the door.

"How's everything going in here, lovies? Did you miss me?" she asks. "I've got some *wonderful* news!"

"You lined up some great sponsors for us?" I ask, excitedly. I know it's silly of me, but for some reason, the idea of surviving the Games is enticing to me.

"Nope," she replies. "Got you some new cage technicians. You're going to love them. They have even more cages than before."

"What happened to our old ones?"

"Nine out of ten people who work in jobs related to the Hunger But Mainly Death Game become terrible drug addicts to deal with the pain, and go live on the streets," she says merrily.

After we're caged, we're brought to the multimedia traincar, where we're going to study footage from old tournaments and get advice from Hagridmitch. While the old tapes are loading, we flip through a few of Pandumb's television channels. It turns out that the Hunger But Mainly Death Games is only one of many examples of the Capitol's incessant demand for child-killing entertainment. There's DieCarly, in which a girl and her friends are killed every week. I guess the lead kids all died in the first episode, so they just have to keep recasting. There's also Spongebob Squarepants, in which a child is molded into the shape of a frightening monster known as 'Spongebob' and then thrown into the sea for crabs to eat. In fact, as far as I can see, there isn't a single show that doesn't incorporate child-death in some way. Even the business shows do, by using stock charts whose highs and lows are charted by a steel sword that inches ever-closer to its child victim as the end of trading nears.

"This really brings me back," says Pita. "My girlfriend who lives in Slum 13 and I always used to watch TV when we were talking on the phone."

"How is that possible?" I ask.

"What do you mean? It's true."

Hagridmitch pipes up from his pooptarp cocoon. "Sure, Neville, sure! An' I have enough self-control ter keep from eatin' eat a two pound bag a' dry pancake mix e'ry night before bed."

"I'm completely serious." Pita says.

"Hagridmitch believes ya, lad."

"Guys, I swear. In fact, she was going to come visit me this week. But then this whole Hunger But Mainly Death Games thing happened, and we broke up. It's so unfair," he says, shaking his head. "You don't need to worry, though. My broken heart is mending. And I think it's time to spread my wings. A lot of women would want a guy like me, you know. Kind, loving, full of handy tarp-skills for when there's kissin' to be done."

"What are you talking about? Why would anybody care about that?"

"When I kiss, Bratniss," he says, raising his eyebrow and giving me a sultry stare, "Things have been known to get...*sloppy.*"

"That's revolting," I say. Luckily, the videos of the tournaments begin to play, and my brain can focus on acts of horrible violence instead of the thought of kissing Pita, thereby averting a self-destruct sequence.

We start at the beginning, with the very first Hunger But Mainly Death Games. It's historic, but it's not one of the most exciting tournaments. That's because for a few years after Games were instituted, nobody could believe they actually existed. They just seemed way too crazy and horrible. So, most of the few tournaments is just kids getting together in groups and saying things to the camera like, "Come on, people. This has clearly gone too far," or, "Use your heads, guys. What is all this senseless violence accomplishing?"

Then, by like the fourth Hunger But Mainly Death Games, everyone started getting into it. This led to some of the most memorable Games, like the one in the middle of the ocean, in which the sacrifices were either given an aquatic battlesuit-exoskeleton or a super-intelligent rideable warjellyfish. It turned out that the jellyfish were able to use chemical signals to attract great white sharks and giant squid to come fight, too. For some reason, there were also a ton of beautiful fireworks, and one short portion that took place on zeppelins, high above the Himalayas. It was so cool and beautiful that you almost forgot it was just kids killing each other in front of a green screen.

We also see some of the lesser-known Games, like the twenty-seventh, which were sponsored by Great Britain. Nothing stood out about the tournament itself, but the cover for the official tournament book that came out after was weird and ugly, like all British covers for young adult books.

We watch tournament after tournament, and they start to blur together. The only thread that connects them is that every year, at least one thing seems to go wrong. There was the year when everyone came down with chicken pox, and because of that toddlers were never used again. The Capitol also decided to do away with the in-game nannies. They didn't really make sense in the first place, come to think of it.

The forty-fourth Hunger But Mainly Death Games was Looney Tune-themed. The viewers were pumped when they saw the Cornucopia filled with anvils and the towering Elmer Fudd Destructo-Bots that patrolled the arena, but it ended up being a bust. More kids died that year from being covered in gallons of paint to make them look like cartoon characters than they did from stupidly tying themselves to a rocket, or not understanding that a crate of ACME TNT blowing up does more than cover your face in black soot.

The list goes on: the Capitol flies everybody to a fire planet, but none of the sacrifices know how to fire-surf. They uses shrink-rays to make everybody tiny, and then puts them inside the bloodstream of a living person, and promise the games will be particularly brutal. Instead, the Sacrifices have a lot of fun learning about the human body. Somewhere along the line, the tournament turns into a big, fun flag football game, and the Gamemakers don't have the heart to remind the kids to kill each other.

After watching highlights from all seventy-three games, I realize two things.

The first is that I'll have to watch out for the sacrifices known as "careers," which is a loose acronym for "the rich kids from Slums 1-3 who train for the Games from birth and usually win." You can count on them to be bigger, stronger, better nourished, and have cool Nike Shox.

Second, I realize I'll have to use some of my free time to go over my rules handbook. Up until now, I was under the impression that every kid *except one* got to win the tournament.

"So, Hagridmitch," I say. "Now that we're done, what kind of advice do you have for us?"

"Advice? Er, lemme think...Well, don't ever—an' I mean *ever*—eat a Bertie Bott's All-Flavored Bean that's colored cat-bladder yellow. That's a sure recipe fer—"

"No, I mean about the tournament. What advice do you have about the *tournament*? The one you fought in and won?"

He looks bewildered.

"What are ye talkin' about? I warn't never in no 'tournament.'"

"That's pretty funny," I say, "Except not to us!" The coffee table is already crashing over his back when I realize, hey, wait a minute, we watched all of the Games but didn't see Hagridmitch once—certainly not standing at the winner's podium. I pause for a moment, and hear a snatch of what Hagridmitch is muttering.

"...They put a bag over me head...took me away, outta my world...wonder how Harry's doin'...why don' he help me..did *he* do this to me?"

I'm beginning to think that maybe we should find someone who actually knows about the Games and ask them some basic questions. I mean, when we were watching those videos, all Oofie did was insist that we pay attention to the kids who managed to die in cool ways. But suddenly, the train grinds to a halt. There's a loud bang, and smoke begins to fill the room. The blast has torn apart the side of the car we're in, and a group of armed men and women storm in. A masked man with a rifle steps forward.

"Bratniss Everclean?" he asks.

"That's me," I manage.

"You're safe, girl. We're with the Pandumb Resistance Front. We're staging the revolt against the Capitol. And we want you to be our leader."

"Really? Oh my—"

“Just kidding,” he says, pulling off his mask to reveal a face slathered in makeup. “My name is Cinnabon, and I’m here to make you gorgeous, girlfriend.”

R-i-i-i-p!

That's the sound my nervous fart makes, as it shoots straight into the face of Vongoria NiceShoes, who's tending to me in the prep room. It's about the seventh time I've done it.

"I'm really sorry about this," I say, blushing. "Sometimes, when I'm anxious, I…you know."

"Don't worry about it, deal!" Vongoria pipes merrily, "In the Capitol, what you're doing is considered polite!"

"Really?" I ask, amazed.

"No, of course not. And if you keep doing it, I'm going to laser your butt shut."

I sigh. So, my quest to find the one place on Earth where girls don't have to hold in their farts all the time must continue. For a moment, I wonder if I'm asking too much of myself. Isn't my plate a little full already? But I banish the thought. I've seen too many of my friends explode from compacted fart-gas for that.

Attendants mill about the room. Dressed in the height of Capitol fashion, they're a strange sight indeed. Working on my toes is Grabulation St. Lil Wayne, whose hair is up in the shape of a fast car. "Vroooooom," he says, every second. Next to him is Skankdumb Dumbstupid, who has a tangle of fibre-optic cables sticking out of her head, each with a miniature satellite on the end. These are the tell-tale signs of a "Livetweeter," a person whose body has been modified to allow constant real-time narration of their existence over the Internet. "Now I'm looking at this weird girl and she's part-creature," she says. "#lmaopoorpeople."

On my left is a woman called Crocs. Her name certainly fits—she's had her head enlarged into the shape of a massive rubber clog, and there are holes all over her face, which show her skull and brain. "Do you want to be like me, sweetie?" she asks. "Do you want to be able to put shoe charms on your face?" She a jams a shiny four-leaf clover pendant into her forehead and falls over dead.

Meanwhile, Vongoria continues her relentless quest to rid my body of hair. All of it must go, she says: my leg hair, my armpit hair, even my thick handlebar mustache. These people, it seems, in their frenzied desire to stand out at all costs, have deemed such things "too normal." But why must they force me to conform to their twisted standards of beauty? I feel the anger rising inside me.

"I see now!" I shout, "You want me to look like that freak!" I point at a woman who has stripped her body of every single hair. The room falls silent.

"I can't believe you'd call me that," the woman says, her lip trembling. "I have a condition called alopecia totalis. My body is unable to produce hair."

"Oh, geez," I say, "Look, I'm really sorry. I didn't—"

"Don't you listen to her, Mary!" says a man who rushes up to her and takes her hands. "You're the most beautiful woman in the world!"

She begins to sob into his shoulder, and then he turns a withering eye towards me. "YOU! Get out! Right this instant!"

"Okay!" I say, unable to believe my luck. I've just been set free from the Hunger But Mainly Death Games! "Goodbye, now!"

"Yeah, nice try," says Vongoria, pulling me back down. "Hold still while we shave the hair off your eyes." Under her breath, she murmurs to herself, "*We should really get a doctor in here to see this.*"

I have to laugh: "doctor." Another one of the nonsense words these Capitol-dwellers pepper their conversations with, like "teeth" or "happiness." No wonder the children of Slum 12 enjoy imitating their odd speech, with its tiny amount of spit and drool, and complete lack of monkey grunts. It's strange—even though I've been observing them for days, I don't have a clue how they warn the rest of the monkey nest when a bird is stealing some of their food or string.

As they work, I begin to wonder what Cinnabon has in store for me. Whatever outfit he comes up with could be the difference between death and what Cinnabon calls "fashion death." Who knows, he might even end up being a sort of spiritual adviser, leading me to start thinking about the big things, and, like, questioning the world around me. That's usually the kind of thing people get into the fashion industry to do.

"Listen closely," Cinnabon suddenly says from behind me, "the outfits I make you will be worn in all the important events—the most important being the Interrogations. As you can probably guess, these fabrics are worth more than either of our lives, even these practice outfits I'm about to give you. If you so much as rip a single fiber in these garments, people close to you will need to be...*erased*."

"Oh my god! I promise to be super carefu—"

"Kidding, kidding. I went down to the morgue, and they're having a ridiculous sale."

I hear the chime of a small bell, and my heart leaps a little—can it be? I glance over at Cinnabon.

"Thank goodness. I was getting famished."

So, the people in the Capitol have afternoon tea, the way we do back in the Crack. I know it's foolish, but I feel a degree of comfort. Tea has always been one of my favorite parts of the day. It's a chance to chat with your loved ones and push your troubles aside, even if only for fifteen minutes. It's only a small similarity that the Crack and the Capitol share, but it makes me think. That maybe, we aren't so different after all. That maybe, we're all victims of the same system. That we could band together to throw off its chains. I'm beginning to think it's not all that crazy—

BANG! The doors to the room swing open. A group of Xeroxes, yoked together like oxen, struggle and pant as they inch their way inside, dragging several massive tanks filled with water from cords around their waists. Everyone in the room has turned their full attention towards the tanks. Or, more specifically, the large grey creatures bumping against the sides. They eye them hungrily.

Cinnabon realizes that I'm confused.

"You poor thing," he says. "You've probably never eaten an entire live manatee every afternoon, have you? Don't worry, I have an extra carving-saw. "

"You're actually going to eat that thing?" I ask, disgusted.

"'Course," he replies, already slugging down rope after rope of manatee blubber, "What else would we do for 'Tee Time?"

"In the Crack, we used to...put some dry pieces of leaves into water..." Even before it's out of my mouth, I know it's a mistake. The whole room bursts into laughter, even the Xeroxes.

I watch my mouth and the rest of 'Tee Time goes off without a hitch. Cinnabon is a pretty nice guy, it turns out. And as we're leaving for our tour of the Capitol, I can't help but ask him, "Cinnabon, what do you have in mind for my outfit tonight?"

He gets this far off look in his eyes as he speaks, "What I have in mind...is the kind of outfit that just might...revolutionize the world...But that's for later. For now, let's go take a look at this marvelous city."

"Wait, do we really have time for sightseeing? I'd rather train, if that's okay." Cinnabon considers it, and I can tell he sees my point.

"Take a left onto that waterslide tube, please," Cinnabon tells the driver. The cab swerves sharply and soon we're riding a wave down a clear tube, outside of which is a shimmering marine environment, somehow. All around us, sea creatures glide through the water, and there are also some giraffes tumbling around.

"These giraffes don't look too healthy to me," I say, as one of their rotting bodies smashes into the glass and tears apart.

"Those aren't normal giraffes, honey, those are sea-giraffes," Cinnabon corrects me. "And don't worry, they're being refreshed right now." He points above us, and up on the surface I can see a barge dumping tons of new giraffes overboard.

"We'll get out here, sir," Cinnabon says, as we pull up in front of the biggest building I've ever seen. It towers over us. Lines of people in their finest clothing waiting to enter stretch as far as the eye can see. At the front doors, a man in a long black frock dabs holy water onto their foreheads. The people cross themselves, and then slide their shoes off before entering. I look up at its massive, neon "Mall of Pandumb" sign in awe.

Cinnabon hands the driver two silver coins and we exit the cab.

"You must think we're monsters," he says, as we step up onto the sidewalk.

"Because of the tip you gave him? I guess it wasn't as much as some people would give, but I think tipping is a matter of personal preference, and I would never judge you for it."

"Oh, honey. That wasn't a tip. Those were coins to put over his eyes right before he kills himself, to assure safe passage into the Deathworld. In the Capitol, we only use cabs and cab drivers once, and then they are required by law to go laserboom."

"Okay, that is pretty monstrous."

"I know, right?" he says, shaking his head sadly. "If only there were something to do about it. If only there could be something like a *savior* who came and *saved us*...perhaps some girl who needed a bit of saving herself, first...perhaps some nice, caring soul could help her escape...escape so she could become a symbol of rebellion and help end these monstrosities..." He winks.

"Are you suggesting—"

"One sec, dear." He taps the Bluetooth in his eye. "Capitol Cab? Yeah, I just got out of a cab number four-four-two and the driver's really taking his sweet time initiating death procedures. Could you laserboom him, please?"

The execution center is next to the food court, so we stop by. The top criminal on Pandumb's Most Wanted is there, having finally been apprehended the week before. She was a well-known scribe, and rose to fame after releasing her first novel. Unfortunately, the book was so criminally bad that the only choice the Capitol had was to burn the book as well as the author.

As she's led down to the fire gallows, a judge lists her crimes. "Having an insipid main character utterly devoid of redeeming qualities—and who is a weak, terrible role model for impressionable fans the world over;"

"Inhumane and unrelenting thesaurus abuse;"

"The implicit promise of action and entertainment, despite an utter inability or criminal unwillingness to provide either;"

"Sappiness levels so high that sap quite literally oozes from the pages, making fingers uncomfortably sticky."

"Writing the book that will end up being the only one some people ever read; and making that book be terrible;"

"For this, and much more, I sentence you, Stephenie Meyer, to death by fire." Executioners in "Fire Squad" t-shirts grab the woman and start marching her down the stairs to the fire pit.

"I'm sick!" she cries as she reaches the top, "I'M SICK!"

That's when the bag goes over her head. This being the Capitol, I'd have expected them to use a high-quality silken bag, or something. But no, the same kind of rotten old potato sack we use for executions in the Slum 12. The crows will get her eyes.

Our tour continues. As we stop at an indoor mall crosswalk, and I look at the "Rebel/Don't Rebel" signal, which from what I can tell is permanently stuck on "Don't Rebel," I notice something peculiar. "Cinna, why is that man walking a naked guy on a leash?"

"Oh, child. The naked one has signed on to be that man's dog. It's practically the most fashionable thing you can do now. Take a close look as they walk past, and you'll see how genius it is."

The naked man catches up to us at that moment, and sees me staring at him. "Bow-*wow*," he says with a sneer.

We reach a large store, bustling with shoppers. "Our first stop," says Cinnabon. "Sacrifices 'R' Us."

"There's an entire *toy* store devoted to us in here?" I ask, incredulously. I don't know if I want to see what's in there..."

"Sweetheart, the sacrifices are the most famous people on the planet right now," says Cinnabon. "You've got to learn to put up with a little bit of adulation. Do feel free to check out the other stores, though."

I glance at the store next to us. The sign in its window reads, "ABERCROMBIE AND FITCH: OUR CLOTHES WORK AS CONDOMS NOW."

"Okay, maybe I will go in the toy store." I say.

"That's the spirit," Cinnabon replies with a mischievous twinkle in his eye. "After all, who says you're too old to play with toys?"

Maybe this won't be so bad. Maybe the toys will portray me in a cool light.

"I didn't know you laid fish eggs," says Cinnabon, reading the back of a playing card.

"What? Give me that!" I say, snatching it away from him. Under the headline "Fun Facts about Bratniss" is a list:

Fact #1: Smells weird

Fact #2: Eats mad boogies.

Fact #3: Favorite activity is guarding her fish eggs that she keeps inside her gills.

I flip the card over to see an illustration of myself squatting in an oily swamp. They've given me with a rat-like tail, which is sticking out of my pants and coiling around a pile of soft, glimmering eggs. I'm baring two fangs at the viewer.

"Why would the Capitol do this to us?" I ask. "None of this is true!"

"Well, I doubt the Capitol would have put it on so much merchandise without fact-checking it," says Cinnabon, handing me the package of something called an "Easybake Bratniss." On the back, it reads, "Just plug her in, spoon her beloved leeches into her mouth, and watch the eggs foam out of her gills! You'll have bowl after bowl of squirming Bratniss-eggs in no time. But beware—if she feels you brush against her leg-spikes, she'll release a noxious protection scent."

I give Cinnabon a withering glare.

"Hey, don't protection-scent the messenger!" he says. "Besides, maybe some monster-people will sponsor you now."

I turn away and begin to scan the aisles. Despite the inaccuracy of my own description, this could be the perfect opportunity for me to learn more about the strengths and weaknesses of my opponents. Besides, I need to find a dark, moist place to lay my eggs.

But as I trawl through aisle after aisle of toys I realize there aren't any toys of the other sacrifices. These are all just toys of *me*. I go back to the front of the store and look at the sign. Sure enough, there in super tiny font after "Sacrifices 'R' Us" is "(Just Bratniss)"

So the Capitol has individualized toy stores for each sacrifice. This is absurd. Can things get any more annoying?

They can. Up at the register, I see *Pita* talking to the clerk! What is he doing here? "Do you have any My Size Bratnisses with realistic kissing-action?" he asks.

"Nah," says the clerk, "the only features in these toys are to make sure they bleed and explode realistically. But you might want to check the Hunger But Mainly Death Games kissing-pillow store."

I can't let him know I'm here. What if he sees me and thinks I'm a walking pillow? I shudder at the thought as I duck into one of the aisles, knocking a few Tickle Me to Death Bratnisses off a shelf.

I can't believe this. Here we are, *shopping*, when I have a death tournament to prepare for, and more importantly than that, an Interrogation to look pretty for. I go tap Cinnabon on the shoulder.

"Cinnabon, I want to leave now. I need to train, you need to start working on my dress, and this place is depressing as hell."

He gives a hearty laugh.

"Bratniss, honey, you're a breath of fresh air. I know exactly how you feel, and I've got just the thing. Follow me!"

Before I can protest, he's grabbed my hand and is dragging me even deeper into the mall. As we get close to wherever he's taking me, he tells me to close my eyes.

"It's *so* like me to dawdle on too long inside the shops and boutiques. But sometimes you've gotta get away from all of that materialism. And enter a winter wonderland. You can open your eyes now, Bratniss."

And there, in front of me, is a morbidly obese man dressed in a Santa costume, sitting in a lawn chair with tinsel taped onto the legs. His girth spills out through the back of the chair and underneath its arms. In some places it's hard to make out where his body ends and the chair begins.

"*Go sit on his lap,*" Cinnabon whispers. "*He'll make all your dreams come true unless you're poor.*"

"Cinnabon, that guy doesn't look okay."

"Don't be silly. He's *Santa*. Santa's always okay."

"Is there a hospital in this mall? Can we take him there?"

"Sweetheart, Santa never leaves his Santa chair. He has elves to wait on him hand and foot! Now go sit in his lap and tell him what you want for Christmas!"

"It's September," I protest. "Not even CVS has its Christmas stuff out yet." Cinnabon isn't having any of it, and picks me up and sets me down on the man's huge stomach.

"Huh? Wha? Soup?" he says, beginning to stir.

Now that I'm up close, I can see that his suit has been bleached pink from the sun.

"H-ho," he says, his eyes still closed, his face inches from mine. "What do you want for Christmas this year, little girl?"

His breath smells like sewage. And he—wait a second, is he...is he *fused to this chair?*

"Sir, are you all right?"

"Elfy!" he calls out. "Elfy write that down! She says she wants...she says...Elfy, isn't it time for my soup?"

Behind the man's chair, there's a small structure made of stiff pastel cardboard, with a sign on top that reads, "Elfy's Magic Xmas Shack." Splayed out at the foot of the doorway is a small skeleton in an elf suit. I look closer and see the skeleton's ankle is chained to a pipe in the shack.

"Did you know," the man whispers, "That I have a little helper named Elfy?"

"What'd I tell you?" says Cinnabon, swinging the gate to the display shut. "Christmas spirit to all, and to all a good night! And, what do you know! We even have time to stop by the Easter Bunny's hutch!"

It's dark when we get back and, up in my room, I try desperately to remember what it even feels like to cut a squirrel in two and make socks out of each half—something, *anything* to remind me of home. And, more importantly, to keep my mind off the quickly-approaching tournament.

But the memories are fading too fast, and all I'm left with is this vivid recollection of pre-school recess when Pita decided to go down the slide face-first and the older boys grabbed onto his sweatpants, causing them to rip off when he went down. Somehow, he didn't notice, and continued happily playing. The swings, the jungle gym, tetherball, you name it and he played it butt-naked that recess.

I can't believe he's the closest person I have to a friend here. Maybe if I had been paired with someone more normal, it would be easier. It certainly doesn't help that the Capitol seems to have brought out the stalkier side of Pita. I have to stay on guard at all times.

THUD. Pita falls from the ceiling and smashes into my floor. "So sorry," he says, pulling a chunk of insulation from his mouth. "There was, uh, something wrong with your ceiling and I was quietly fixing it. Didn't want to disturb you, m'dear."

If only he weren't like this. But how do you get the creepiest boy on earth to act normal? It's not like you can just *ask* someone to be normal.

Or can you?

"Pita. Drop the act. Right now," I say, snapping my fingers.

"What? This is how I am," he says, adjusting his video camera. "Big weirdo, in big, weird love with my lovely lady. Hold still, this thing won't zoom off of your boobs. Mind of its own, this camera."

I sigh. "Pita, can't you at least *act* like a normal human being? For a little bit? No creepy stuff for 10 minutes, okay?"

And you know what? It seems to work. Pita turns off the camera, and sits down next to me. I have no idea whether I've actually gotten through to him, but right now, I don't even care. I just want someone to talk to.

So we talk, and it's actually kind of enjoyable. We talk about the Crack, and our families, and how maybe it's kind of unfair to make teenagers kill each other on national television. On top of that, it actually turns out that we have some things in common! He may have black hair and I may have brown hair, but we both have hair. His mom is a sex robot and mine is psychopathic bread-kisser, but hey, close enough. It even turns out he and I are the same species!

Okay, so we don't have that much in common, but at least he isn't acting like a complete gross-out weirdo now.

"You know, growing up, I always respected you," he says. "I'm sure what happened to your dad was a hard burden to carry throughout junior high…and how hard geography class was for you…"

There, a hundred billion miles away from our hometown, only a day removed from almost certain death, I'm finding out that this boy who has plagued me my entire childhood really isn't such a bad guy. Beneath his yucky, video camera-wielding, hole-in-the-shower-looking-through exterior is a down-to-earth, in some ways level-headed boy who has been sentenced to death like me. So, I start opening up even further. And by opening up, I mean I'm telling secrets. Who my first crush was. Why girls go to the bathroom in groups. Then, as I'm about halfway through explaining the danger of stall dragons, I realize how dimly lit the room has become.

"Hey, what's happening?" I ask. "I didn't think they'd have power shortages here in the Capitol."

"You're right, it's so strange," he murmurs. "But I was getting the feeling that all that light was a little *impersonal.*" He sweeps back his arm, and I see that we're now surrounded by candles. Pita claps his hands twice. To my surprise, my closet swings open and three…loaves of bread walk out? Wearing little pairs of sunglasses? Their mouths open, and—

"Oompa, loompa, doopity-doo," they sing, as they march around me in a circle. Then their sunglasses shoot off, and they look up at me, with little cameras where their eyes should be. "…KISS-KISS-KISS-KISS-KISS-KISS-KISS."

I fly out of the room, gasping for air. Behind me, he yells out, "Is it something my breadbots said?" As I'm running through the halls, I have a very disturbing realization. And it's not that just that Pita is somehow incapable of not trying to get me to date him. It's that he's much smarter than I thought, at least in a bread-robotics sort of way.

I don't have long to ponder this, because I get a text from Oofie: "time 4 trayning betch."

Within seconds, I'm teleported into the official training facility, along with the other twenty-three sacrifices. They haven't given anyone time to prepare. Some are still in their underwear. One is right in the middle of peeing. He makes no effort to stop. "If you guys can stop as soon as you've started, more power to you," he says, shrugging.

But no one really cares, because we're all astounded by the training center we've suddenly found ourselves in. It's *beautiful.* It's like a court, covered in hard, shiny wood. At each end of the court is an iron ring, beneath which a foot or so of pearly white netting extends. Vibrant colored lines snake along the wood at unpredictable angles. Next to one such line is a little sticker on the floor that says "Free Throw Line."

"Get as much training in while you can," a voice announces via intercom, "A local women's volleyball team has this court reserved for 4PM."

But, wait, it's already 3:40. They're only giving us twenty minutes to train today? A measly twenty minutes to begin our preparation for the Hunger *But Mainly Death Games*? Come on, wouldn't more training at least make for better television? But apparently that means nothing to the Gamemakers, or the ludicrously tall, spandex shorts-wearing women stretching on the sides. They glare at us impatiently, volleyballs balanced atop their heads.

A whistle sounds, and the other sacrifices sprint to stations throughout the facility, above which hang banners explaining each station's function.

There are lots of options: "Ducking;" "Maybe You Should Act Like a Tree;" "Is This Water Brown or Clear?" But before I can decide between "What Does a Knife Look Like?" and "Poop Bomb: Yes, Seriously," a big, strong, veiny adult hand grabs me. It's Oofie. She's wrangled Pita up, too.

"Don't bother with the stations," she says. "Twenty-three out of twenty-four sacrifices who rely on them end up dead. I've managed to get you guys something special: your own personal trainer."

Suddenly, a massive shadow looms over us and, all I can smell is sun tan lotion. I start to gag. When I turn and look at him and I start to gag even harder. His skin is golden-brown, but not in the good way. Not even in the Snooki way. It's over-tanned and leathery, like something you'd peel off of a roasted chicken. His muscles jiggle around under the skin and each several-inch long baby-step he takes appears to be causing him a lot of pain. He wears nothing but shiny white boots and tight white spandex pants.

"Meet Malibu, former Pandumb Gladiator, and now an official Hunger But Mainly Death Games trainer," Oofie says, beaming.

Malibu tries to speak, but he's struggling. His face is set in place like concrete. Little injection holes in his neck dilate as he breathes. Finally, he musters a few gravelly words, "Bring...turkey sandwich...Oofie?"

"You'll get your payment once training is *complete*," she says, before turning to us. "Now, children, Mr. Malibu will be teaching you today. And if you pay attention, you might learn a thing or two about dying with honor."

And with that Oofie is gone. Pita takes this as his cue, "All right, first thing's first: the kissing station. We need to train there if we want to survive!"

"Wait…kid..." says Malibu, audibly pained to be speaking, "more useful stuff…learn first."

With that I instantly take a liking to Malibu. Yes, he may look ridiculous and yes, he may be hardly able to move or speak, and yes, on top of all that, I can clearly see the catheter snaking down his spandex pants and into his boots, but the man actually seems to have a shred of common sense.

"First thing…teach you," Malibu begins, "Tug...o' War."

Okay. So this guy might even be a bigger idiot than Pita.

"Can't stress…importance…win games with rope."

Even Pita questions the logic of this, "Mr. Malibu, are you sure there aren't any other...*slightly more important stations* we could go to? I hear there's a snuggling station out back. It's integral that Bratniss and I know how to use our body heat efficiently."

"You kids want be…Gladiator Champion…or not?" Malibu says. Then something pops into his head. He slowly peers around to see if anyone is watching us, then leans in and says, "You kids want…learn something really dangerous?"

At this point, I'm up for anything. Pita agrees and Malibu tells Pita to go get his gym bag. When Pita leaves Malibu turns to me and says, "You have…extra Botox?"

"Uh, no."

"What…about syringes? Fine…if empty."

"Mr. Malibu, I don't—"

I'm cut off by Pita's scream. I look over at him. He's staring into Malibu's bag, clearly terrified.

"There's a GUN in here!" he shouts.

"Yes…" Malibu begins, walking over and placing the gun into Pita's shaking hands. "I show you…dodge bullet."

Malibu clicks the safety off of the gun and motions for Pita to shoot him.

"Simple…kids," Malibu says, "stand in front…gun…just jump...when you hear it...FIRE!"

BANG!

The bullet flies through Malibu's head and he falls to the floor.

A ghost-faced Pita looks at the smoking pistol in his hand and drops it. The gun clatters against the floor and fires—BANG BANG BANG—all into Malibu. Greenish-red, sun tan lotion-scented ooze begins pouring out of him.

I've never been this close to a dead person before, and it's a harrowing experience. I try to pick up Malibu's gun to put it back in his gym bag, out of respect, but the second I reach down for the gun it fires again, this time smack dab into Malibu's thigh. Hmm, maybe I should test this. I kind of fake like I'm about to grab the gun and pull my hand back at the last sec—BLAM—the gun fires again. But this time it misses. The shot is way off, into the rafters. Ha, nowhere near—wait, no, it actually just unhinged a big electronic scoreboard which is now sailing downward in 3…2…CRUNCH. The scoreboard cuts Malibu's body clean in half.

Not bad, I think. *Now if I can just practice it a few more times, it'll be second nature in the arena.* A gong sounds and the intercom crackles, "That's it, kids, training is over. Over forever. Time to kill each other. Whoops sorry—in a few hours, I mean, haha, obviously please don't start—"

But the announcer is too late. A gigantic boy from Slum 1 has already torn off the head of another sacrifice. The rest of the sacrifices gape at him, in awe. He is tall. We're talking like puberty tall.

And, like most boys who have gone through puberty, he has a robotic laser eye, one of his arms looks like some sort of rocket launcher, and most terrifyingly, his voice has changed. When he talks...it's like hearing a *dad* talk. Gradually, I begin to hear his name whispered by the sacrifices around me. *Scar*. And then, as the whispers continue, I hear his last name. Scar *Humphrey*. That's...well, actually, he should probably just go by his first name if he wants to sounds scary.

One by one, the sacrifices are ushered out of the facility and into a side room, where they each show the judges how dangerous they are. Finally, my turn comes and I am ushered into a room with white walls and a white table in the middle. On top of the table is a small chocolate chip cookie with a note next to it: "If you can wait fifteen minutes without touching the cookie, we will bring you three more cookies."

A cookie? How can withstanding the urge to eat a cookie possibly give an accurate impression of our skills in the arena?

Shaking my head in disbelief, I look over at the window from which the judges are monitoring me. And I realize that they are a group of toddlers. They stare back at me, some drooling, some wiping their noses on their sweater sleeves, diapers bulging in their Oshkosh B'Gosh overalls. Several are in the middle of a nap.

That's it. The lack of proper training is bad enough, but to find out that the judges are *toddlers*? That's too much. It's time to do something drastic. In an instant, I know what I must do.

The judges said I shouldn't eat the cookie. But they didn't say I couldn't stab it in the face with a big old butcher knife. So I walk over to the rack of knives conveniently located next to the cookie table—you know, where they are in most social science experiments—and slide out a monster of a blade. We're talking serrated edges, serrated handle, and a little buzz saw feature that really isn't necessary for what I'm about to do…

BZZZZ. I use the buzz saw feature anyway. Because screw this cookie. THUNK. The saw-knife slams through the cookie and kills it in f***ing half.

That gets the judges' attention.

They leap up from their seats and paw at the glass wall. Even through that thick glass I can hear their pained cries. One toddler crumples to the floor in tears. Another has been driven so insane that he starts giving *himself* a spanking.

As I'm dragged out, I stare at the teary-eyed judges. *Yes*! I think. *I nailed my audition.* Kiss your cookie goodbye, stupid idiot babies.

But maybe I'm the stupid idiot. I just upset the very people who will give me my danger score, which is some...measure...that means...something...And getting the *wrong* danger score...Well, I'm not sure what it could do, really. Whatever the case, it's still insulting to have babies judging us.

I'm taken to a small chamber where the rest of the sacrifices are waiting. I begin to walk out when Pita yells after me, "Where are you going? The judges are about to announce the danger scores!"

"*Already*? I was there like two minutes ago."

"Shh, now they're halfway through!"

We gather round the TV in rapt silence. On screen is the judges' art teacher from daycare. "Remember, the judges worked very hard on these!" she begins. "Okay. Next up, Bratniss Everclean. Now, I don't think you'll be surprised to hear that we've been learning about Thanksgiving over the last few weeks," she chuckles, holding up a piece of orange construction paper. There, in the middle of a crayon hand-tracing turned into a turkey, is my score.

Three million. Plus infinity.

Three million plus infinity. Everyone in the room sits in stunned silence. Except for Hagridmitch, who, as always, is mumbling something drunkenly. "Three million points…that's almost enough right there to win the Tri-Wizard cup. But that cup is Harry's ter win, innit? Not Hermione's. Some kinder trickery's afoot, and I think I kin guess who: Vol—"

"Don't you say it!" hollers Oofie.

"Ah, yer right, yer right…what was I thinkin'? All us adults are serposed to be idiotically superstitious. I meant He-Who-Must-Not-Be-"

"Shut your fat mouth!" shouts Oofie, chasing him out of the room.

"Best be off now!" he says, ducking out, "Cheers, Hermione! Stay away from Mandrakes, Neville!"

And now that that's over with: three million plus infinity. It's almost the highest score you can get, right after three million and infinity plus one. Of course, no one's even cracked one million before. From what I can remember, the highest score to date was an eleven, and all the sacrifices just ganged up on that kid and killed him in the opening minutes. But the sacrifices this have probably forgotten about last year's Games. Hopefully, they'll steer clear of me, and then I can sneak off and hide in the forest. It's an old trick I learned from cross country meets: when in doubt, wait everything out in the middle of the woods, and come back at the end with some fake sweat painted onto your body, and all of the Dorito dust brushed off of your hands and face.

Now that I've figured out my strategy, it's time to turn my attention to something that may be even more important: the Interrogations. Oofie's told me that they're a chance for us to impress sponsors by wearing a stunning outfit, because fashion is a vital part of the Games. Makes sense, I guess.

Okay, it doesn't make any sense, but, whatever, I'm excited to wear something cool. I think back over some of my favorite outfits from tournaments past. One year, a girl had a perfectly-scaled replica of the Arena wrapped around her, with twenty-four beetles running through it, each wearing a miniature version of their respective sacrifice's outfit. Unfortunately, her designer didn't realize that they were parasitic zombie beetles. By the time she got called up for her interview, she was little more than a dusty skeleton filled with fat, sleepy insects. Another time, a girl's designer broke into the pyramid that held the preserved corpse of Lady Gaga, who was a fashionable musician before the Dark Days. They made her body into a beautiful, screaming cape. Of course, the screaming meant that Lady Gaga's evil spirit had been awakened. But, my word, the *cape* was dazzling.

Not that I'd want outfits like those. But I guess they're further examples of how incredibly entertaining the Games are, as long as you aren't in them.

I turn to consult with Cinnabon, but he's nowhere to be seen. Oh, good. He must have sealed himself away to make sure that whatever I wear is perfect. I guess I'll take this time to prepare for the Games on my own terms: by thinking over and over again about how much I don't want to die.

When I get back to my room, a weary Cinnabon is waiting for me with bloodshot eyes. I can't believe it—he's stayed up all night working on my costume!

"Close your eyes," he orders.

It takes every ounce of self-restraint I have to obey. I want to see my outfit. I can't imagine what this mad genius has come up with for me and I want to see it right n—

"You can open your eyes, now."

I am not pretty. I am not beautiful.

I am dressed in a knock-off, child-sized Batman costume. The Halloween store price tag is still attached, and the costume doesn't even have an actual Batman insignia. The black "bat" is just a dog.

"Goddamnit, Cinnabon," I say.

"Is that a happy goddamnit?" he asks with a grimace.

"You forgot that the Interrogations were today, didn't you?"

"No! Of course not! Believe me, it may not look like much right now, but when you're onstage it transforms into—" My glare cuts him short.

"All right, I did forget, Bratniss. But it was only because I was so anxious to make you a great dress that I completely lost track of time! I was so engulfed in my craft, and—" Again, my glare cuts him short.

"Okay, it was because I went to a huge drugs party."

A drugs party? What does he think he's been employed by the Capitol to do—go to drugs parties all the time? Shit, I guess that is what he thinks. Either that, or he's not a very reliable person.

"Bratniss, I'm sorry. I kept thinking I would be able to leave the party early and make something for you. And I think I did, at one point. But now I can't remember where I put it. I should never have snorted all that glitter. Ke$ha's just so damn pushy!"

Oh, well. I guess part of me was looking forward to becoming a god-like figure of awe for the entire country based on one dress, but maybe that was a little unreasonable. And knowing how useless sponsors are, it's not like I have to try to impress anybody. At least I'll have one other person to share my embarrassment with: Pit—

Ah, crud. Pita floats into the room in a strikingly tailored suit with a faintly shining map of the night sky sewn into it.

"I'll tell you, Bratniss," he says happily, "Dressing fashionably may be expensive, but you can't argue with the comfort! I feel so confident! In fact, I think—AH, BATMAN!" he shouts, finally noticing my outfit. "I'm sorry I dressed up, Batman! Please don't eat me!"

"It's only me, Pita," I say. "Cinnabon forgot to make my outfit. Come on, we've got to go to the Interrogations."

The 'Peace'keepers show up to transport us, and before I know it, I'm on the stage of the Royal Capitol Theatre Sponsored by Red Bull®, a massive space usually reserved for productions of Shakespeare's classics, like "Romeo & Dying in the Hunger But Mainly Death Games," and "Charlie and the Chocolate Factory." Funny, how the place people come to celebrate some of the greatest human achievements is also the place they come to indulge their cruel, bloodthirsty side. But that's adults for you: hypocritical jerks.

The sacrifice seating is a special screened-off row of bleachers high above the stage. In fact, from what I can tell, where we're sitting is actually outside the stadium. A biting wind emanates from the clouds several feet above our heads.

I can just make out the Capitol people seated comfortably in the crowd far below, with servants tending to their every need.

"Enemas! Get your rich-person enemas, here!" a man with a big vacuum-ey hose looped over his shoulder yells. Various Capitol-dwellers are bent over in their velvet seats, clamoring for his attention: "Put it here, enema man! Put it here!"

Unbelievable. The Capitol can afford to give their citizens in-seat enemas, and yet we, the people who are about to die, are stuck sitting on cold metal bleachers, shivering and trying to duck out of the way of passing planes.

But as I look around at the other sacrifices shivering here with me, I feel an odd sense of solidarity. In a few short hours, we will be competitors. But, for now, we are teammates, and we are in this together. All of us, from Slum 12, all the way down to...Slum 4?

What the heck? Why aren't the career slums up here?

Hey, there they are, getting out of a stretch Hummer limo in front of the stage and being escorted to a luxurious private balcony! The girls are wearing awesome prom dresses, and the guys have cool accessories, like top hats and canes! The crowd roars in approval.

Leading the way is an obnoxiously pretty girl in a dazzling red dress. You can tell it's expensive and nice because it has the word "Juicy" emblazoned on the butt.

"Glamorrhea! Glamorrhea!" yells a man off to the side of the red carpet, "Can I get your autograph?"

She stops and smiles, and then has her chauffeur spit in the man's face.

And there's Scar! I can see his rocket launcher gleaming from here. A man squeezes through the crowd and thrusts a mic into Scar's face: "Scar, quick question! I'm from TMZ, and I want to know what you say to the rumors that you were recruited by Slum 1, and illegally transferred there from Slum 2!"

The crowd gasps. Slum 2 sacrifices are usually the unmemorable sidekicks of the kids from Slum 1. Scar stares at the pale little man and then motions offstage. Moments later, someone tosses him a football. He deftly turns, and heaves it in a perfect spiral, far off into the distance. The entire crowd cheers and instantly forgets the recruiting violation because, come on, *sports*.

Following them are Emily and Dylancobra, who look like smaller, less pretty versions of the Slum 1 sacrifices. But the crowd oohs and aahs when they hold up pictures of themselves standing with Glamorrhea and Scar.

"What are they like?" one woman yells, with tears streaming down her face. "Let me touch you!"

The last out of the limo are the sacrifices from Slum 3, whose citizens are known for their proficiency at practical jokes. The girl, whose name isn't announced for some reason, points towards the chest of a man in the front row, as if there's something on his shirt. When he looks down, she pulls out a bat and whacks him in the side of the head. The boy, P'rank, has a cap gun loaded with fart-caps. Every few seconds, he puts it near his butt and pulls the trigger, to waves of rapturous laughter.

They are shown to their seats, a set of six golden thrones. Next to each throne crouches an attendant holding grapes to dangle into the occupant's mouth. They sit down, Glamorrhea has her chauffeur spit into her grape dangler's face for good measure, and then the lights dim.

The stadium goes silent as a drumroll begins, before ending spectacularly with the appearance of Nero Flickabooger, the storied Hunger But Mainly Death Games Interrogator.

On the gargantuan Jumbotron video board which, from where I'm sitting, is about the size of quarter, I can see him begin his routine.

"Good evening, ladies..." he says, whipping his head dramatically, splashing everyone in the first few rows with makeup, "...and gentlemen. And welcome, welcome, to the 74th—"

"Do the head thing!" someone shouts.

Nero seems tickled. "Oh, surely you don't want to see me do the *head* thing!"

"YES! YES WE DO!" come agitated cries from throughout the stadium.

"If you insist!" he says, and then rips his head off of his shoulders and starts juggling it along with several Vidalia onions.

"Hey, Nero!" the head calls out as it sails through a flaming hula hoop, high in the air. "What did the sacrifice say to the other sacrifice?"

Nero's body shrugs and taps its foot impatiently.

"Help! I'm dying! Because you killed me!" the head replies, landing back on Nero's neck.

A laugh track plays as a metallic voice booms over the speakers, "LAUGH NOW."

The audience breaks out into uncontrollable laughter.

"LAUGH STOP," the voice says. And just like that, the Interrogations have begun.

"Darling, you are simply fantastic!" Nero belts out, before Glamorrhea can even get out of her throne to come to the stage.

She takes this as her cue and saunters over. Nero kisses her on both cheeks, and then both cheeks of her face, too.

"Hiiii, Nero," she brays. "And helloooo, Pandumb!" The crowd roars its approval.

"Why is it that you're so beautiful and perfect?" Nero asks.

"Probably because my dad got me this sick boob job for my sixteenth birthday."

"Parents are so important, aren't they? Now, tell me, what's your strategy for winning the Hunger But Mainly Death Games?"

"I'm going to be an evil, catty bitch to anyone I don't like."

"How wonderful, dear!" Nero beams. "How wonderful and honorable. Do you have anything you'd like to say to the crowd before you go?"

"You're all ugly and you'll never find husbands."

"Glamorrhea, everyone!" Nero shouts. "The beautiful, incandescent Glamorrhea!"

As soon as she's offstage, everything goes black, and a song with a thundering bass line begins to play. A spotlight locks onto Scar, who walks onstage rapping: "You are now watchin' the throne, don't let me into my zone!"

Behind him, a video screen unfurls from the rafters. In between images of volcanoes erupting and lightning crashing, we see flashes of Scar. There he is, dunking a basketball and smashing the rim onto the fans behind it; knocking a soccer ball through the goalkeeper on a penalty kick; hitting a massive grand slam that causes the stands to collapse; and helping out at a local soup kitchen, but still managing to look pretty tough.

"You are now watchin' the throne, don't let me into my zone! Don't let me into my zone! I'm definitely in my zone!"

"Oh, no! Don't do it, folks!" Nero yells theatrically. "Don't let this unstoppable killing machine into his zone!"

But it's too late, I guess?

"RAAAAAA!" Scar screams. "I am in my zone! Do you hear that? RAAAAAA!"

Then the music cuts out, the lights come back on, and Scar plops down in his Interrogation chair.

"It's such an honor to have you here, Scar. We're all huge fans, and I'm gonna go ahead and ask you what everyone is wondering right now: what are your plans for after the Games?"

"Well," Scar begins, taking a big bite out of a protein bar, "I'd like to take some time to give back to the community that made me so strong and bloodthirsty. That's why I've started The Scar Foundation. It's all about leveling the playing field, and, let's be honest, it's going to look amazing on a college application. We focus on underprivileged rich kids."

"That is simply amazing. It's so rare to find a young man who—"

"Hate to interrupt you, big guy," says Scar, rising from his chair. "But I've got a 7PM. Golf lessons."

"Oh, of course, of course, don't let us keep...oh, okay, so he's already gone! Scar, everybody!"

Nero looks down at a notecard. "Next, we have the sacrifices of Slum 2. They say they'd like to be interrogated together, and that...only a hero can save us? I'm not sure what that means, and I don't think a dual interrogation is necessarily allowed by—"

But Nero is cut short by the opening chords of Nickelback's "Hero," which Emily and Dylancobra sing soulfully as a montage of pictures of themselves with Glamorrhea and Scar rolls behind. Looking closely, I can see that some of the pictures are just of Glamorrhea and Scar with Emily or Dylancobra photoshopped into the background.

After it ends, the stadium is eerily silent, until Nero starts clapping firmly.

"Bravo, bravo," he says, wiping away a tear. "I think I speak for all of us when I say, that was *stunning*. It really brought the tragedy of all of this home, the tragedy that both Glamorrhea and Scar can't win. If only we had some delightful merry pranksters to alleviate this pain."

Nero is in luck, because up next is the girl from Slum 3, who regales the audience with the story of the time she got her hands on three pigs, numbered them 1, 2, and 4, and set them loose in her school, while she shot everything up with an assault rifle. The crowd can't get enough of it, and a steady stream of laughter-induced pee flows down from the seats. She continues by describing an "old party goof" of hers: when people pass out at parties, she takes a sharpie and draws a dotted line around their neck to make cutting their head off easier.

The pee flows faster and harder, so much so that the stadium enema man slips on the pee and tumbles down the steps, cracking his skull open. This only increases the laughter, and more and more pee gushes down, turning his body this way and that. As the girl from Slum 3 leaves the stage, she is treated to a rousing standing ovation. But when she sits down, she surprises everyone by letting out an ear-shattering fart. Her face turns crimson, and she reaches beneath her seat and pulls out a fart machine.

"Aww, yeah!" shouts P'rank, popping up in the back of the stadium, holding a remote control. "PRANKBOY IS IN DA HOUSE!"

He runs through the aisles getting high fives. If there's one thing the citizens of the Capitol find funnier than horrible violence, it's fart noises. No one has any pee left, so they switch over to poop instead. P'rank masterfully poopboards onstage and takes the opportunity to show off his entire repertoire, which includes, among other fart-things, running around in a pair of shoes that make farting noises with every step he takes, a fartkazoo, a small jar of fart putty you must smush your fingers into just to make it stop farting, a Fart Boy portable gaming console, and a clay model of a butt into which P'rank pours vinegar and baking soda.

Nero is on his knees by the end of it. "Ooh! Ooh! Stop, please stop!" he begs, pounding the ground with his fists.

P'rank steps up, slides the mic out of his hand, and then looks around slyly. He raises it to his lips and says, "Fart."

Several people in the crowd instantly drop over dead. Amongst the surviving laughers is a red-faced Nero, who finally manages to snatch the mic away from P'rank and gasp out, "Well there you have them! This year's Hunger But Mainly Death Games sacrifices! Good night, everyone!"

Streamers cascade down from the ceiling as a guy with a headset rushes out from backstage and whispers something into Nero's ear. Nero rolls his eyes and mutters, "*We have to do all of them?*"

The guy with the headset nods.

"Oh, fine. Line 'em up."

The rest of us are hustled down to the stage, where Nero sits scowling. Crap, I was really banking on getting a detailed understanding of each of my competitors here. What was I thinking when I skipped those mixers where "Get to know your fellow sacrifices" mixers, where everyone got together and explained their weaknesses? I'll have to try my best to glean what I can from their appearances.

But it's difficult, since Nero manages only a few perfunctory words to each of them.

"Hello. Goodbye."

"When I was your age...well, never mind. Next!"

"Cool wheelchair, kid."

Okay, I'll have to focus on a handful of sacrifices and hope that they're somehow the ones who end up playing an important role in the Games. Let's see:

There's the girl from Slum 5, who has a fork cleanly lodged in her head. I miss her name, but I'm pretty confident that it's "Forkface." And something tells me that this girl is *smart*. I'm not sure what it is. It's definitely not the song she keeps singing: "Take fork out, put fork in! That's how me me Forkface win!" But there's a spark in her small, dull eyes that you can't miss.

Then there are these feral kids from Slum 8, who were raised by wolves, and whom I've got this weird feeling about. I don't know, there's just something about them that tells me they are going to be supremely important down the line.

There's also Roo, a tiny sacrifice from Slum 11, who, from what I can tell, was born with a tiny pouch on her stomach for carrying her young, and little velvet flaps under her arms that let her glide from tree to tree. She's the cutest thing I've ever seen. "I can roll into an armadillo ball, so don't count me out!" she says to Nero's back.

Her male counterpart, Bear, doesn't share her bubbly personality, but wows the crowd with his thick, black pelt, his lumbering frame, and his ability to balance a ball on top of his nose.

And then, just like that, it's my turn. As Nero walks toward me, I look down at my felt utility belt and my cardboard batarangs. And suddenly, I think that maybe, just maybe, Cinnabon knew what he was doing. After all, who is Batman, anyway? He's the Dark Knight! The Caped Crusader! The only ray of light in the darkness that is Gotham! And he's just the superhero to show these people, every last one of them, that Bratniss Everclean is not a name to be taken lightly.

I step into the spotlight, and face the crowd.

"WHERE'S JOKER!" I growl.

"Oh," Nero says, backing away from me. "Disgusting. Dear God, please get off the stage."

I'm strapped down to a gurney and carted away immediately. That could have gone better. As I'm being wheeled away, I catch a glimpse of Pita dropping something as he walks past Nero. As soon as it hits the floor, he rushes to grab it, but Nero gets there first, and holds up a small notebook for everyone to see.

"Now, now, what do we have here?" he crows.

"Not my diary!" Pita gasps. "I mean, not my journal! It's a journal!"

"That's odd," says Caesar, pulling a thick shiny book from his pocket. "Then why is it called "Lisa Frank's My First Diary?"

"It doesn't matter what it's called. I write journaly things in there. Whatever, you'll never guess my password!"

Caesar types something into a little keypad on the front of the book.

"Is it…HORSES?" he asks.

"Darnit!" Pita says, as the diary flies open.

"Ooh, la la! Today's entry! How delicious!" Nero says, and then begins to read: "'Dear Diary, Today was the best day of my life. Because today is the day I started dating Bratniss Everclean."

What. The. Heck. Is. Going. On. I. Might. Have. To. Murder. Pita. Right. Here. And. Now.

Damage control, damage control. I have to do something to divert attention from Pita's insane lie, and fast. I can't let everyone think we're an actual couple. And not because it's embarrassing. I don't care what these people think about me. But I do care about what Pita thinks. He's already proven himself to be nothing short of insane when it comes to liking me. Mix in a little positive reinforcement here, a few mixed signals there, and toss us both into the Games, and who can predict how he'll act?

It's too late, though. The crowd roars its approval. One Capitol man screams out, "This is the cutest, most adorable thing *everrrr*!"

Some woman yells, "High school couples are meant to be together forever!"

Another woman says, "Soon you will have a baby!" More faceless voices join in.

"The baby comes from inside you!"

"Have you seen that movie *Alien*?"

"You are with the boy you love FOREVER now!"

I guess this is what happens when a society replaces all of its universities with state-sponsored *Us Weekly* Re-Education Centers.

This isn't how it's supposed to be. When you get your first boyfriend, it's supposed to be a magical experience. Birds are singing, harps are playing, and the Internet is running smoothly so that he can ask you to be his girlfriend through whatever instant messaging program you're using. But this? Having someone crazy try to make me their girlfriend by lying on national television? (And, yes, I promise he's lying. I'm not being an unreliable narrator, here. I haven't been holding anything back from you. Except for the bathroom scenes.)

"Well, that's all the time we have," Nero says, as he reaches out to shake Pita's hand. But he stops, looks at his watch and pulls his hand back. "Whoops, running late. Silly me."

"No worries," Pita begins, beaming, "It's been great speaking with you, Mr.—"

SHOOMPF. Pita falls through the trap door beneath him.

And with that, the Black Eyed Peas are immediately teleported back on stage.

But I'm not interested in listening to that quiet Native American one sing his new solo album. My mind is on one thing, and one thing only: finding Pita and putting an end to this. And then checking my Facebook profile to make sure he hasn't hacked in and accepted his own Relationship request.

But when I get back to the training center, I can't find him anywhere. I've really got to make this quick, so I can do some solemn reflecting about the Games. After all, this is the night before the tournament. I'll definitely need to start planning that escape I've been meaning to make for weeks. But I think finding Pita and having a fight with him will really help me stop procrastinating about it.

I search and I search. I look underneath beds, in ventilation shafts, and I even check inside a few of those comically large birthday cakes lying around. I'm running out of time. But as night turns to day, I still haven't found Pita, and I have no choice but to give up. I walk back into my room and angrily kick a pillow off the top of a pile. Strange light pours out, and I can hear the muted beeps of a sonar machine. I poke my head in. Maybe the submarine commander who must be inside can use that sonar to help me locate—oh, it's a pillow-fort stalking command center. And you can probably guess who's captain of *this* ship.

"PITA!" I shout, kicking aside another pillow.

"Hey! That's one of my…uh, *learning center's* main structural supports!" he shouts back, while trying to obscure the hand-drawn map he's working on, labeled 'Where Bratniss Is.' "What are you trying to do, have all these blankets and maybe a couch cushion fall on me?"

"What do you think you were doing during the Interrogations?" I yell. "You had no right to say that!"

"It's okay, sweetyboopkins. Pitabear is sorry to have revealed our little secret, but it's time for us to be brave. Time for us to stand up to the culture that won't let us declare our love. I know it seems wrong, a boy and a…*girl.*"

"No, you idiot! You had no right to say we that we're dating! If you want me to be your girlfriend, you have to ask me! And I have to say yes!"

"Oh!" he exclaims, his eyes lighting up. "Bratniss, will you be my—"

"No! No, I won't! Because I don't like you! And even if I did, I wouldn't date you because *we're about to be in a death tournament!* We may have to kill each other! Has that not registered in your brain yet?"

He adjusts his pants uneasily. "Hmm, kind of regretting the decision to wear whipped cream boxers right now..."

"Listen to me!" I snap. "Drop all of this right now, and let me focus on the Games!"

He looks up at me ruefully. "Bratniss, what you've shown me is that your teenaged brain still isn't fully-developed. In fact, you'd probably rather be with some vampire, or something. But he won't treat you the way I will, Bratniss. And, were I a lesser boy, I'd let you learn that the hard way. But I can't. I can't let you get your heart broken right in the middle of the Games." He stands up, his voice growing stronger. "So, no! I won't stop!" He looks down at his watch. "Look at the time! 12:10PM! *Happy one day and thirty-five minute anniversary, baby*!"

12:10? That can't be right! If it's past noon, that means the Hunger But Mainly Death Games started ten minutes ago! *Oh, when will these terrifying twists stop wreaking havoc on my life*?

But before I can do anything, Oofie bursts through the roof access and yells, "COME WITH ME IF YOU WANT TO DIE!"

The next few moments are a blur. As the trapdoor opens beneath me and I fall through the floor, and then fall through more trapdoors in each room I land in, I find myself wondering why they rely on trapdoors so much here, and couldn't they have the trapdoors link directly to one another instead of dumping me into small rooms that only seem to serve as anterooms for the next trapdoor.

But I have other things to worry about right now. I'm late for The Hunger But Mainly Death Games! Surely that comes with some form of punishment. I mean, what if they kill us? What if they just up and kill us before we even have the opportunity to be thrown into the arena and killed?

I land in what appears to be the floor underneath the arena, because I can see some roots dangling down. Oofie steps out of the shadows, pulls my face up to hers and says, "If anyone in that arena or any one of the millions of people watching on national television notices that you're late, the agency is taking my cut. If that happens, I'm going back in time, drinking some reverse aging juice, getting picked for the Seventy-Fourth Hunger But Mainly Death Games, and killing you myself."

Then I realize, Hey, aren't we supposed to be outfitted with games uniforms and get certain provisions for the—SHOOMPF. Another trapdoor! Damnit! This one's in the ceiling but still, come on, what ever happened to normal doors?

When I open my eyes, I discover I'm in a lush green field. Around me birds chirp, and I can smell the sweet scent of robotic pine. For a moment, I'm transported back to the idyllic summers in Slum 12 I had as a child. But the time for flashbacks is over. Sometimes, you need to actually let the plot move forward.

I look over my shoulder and see Pita, who's a little freaked out, but still managing to do the sign language for "I love you" at me. Behind him, maybe 100 meters away, are the other sacrifices. Weirdly, they're all just kind of milling around a big table covered in food and supplies. This must be the—

"Hey, everybody! This is your announcer speaking! Before we begin the Seventy-Fourth Hunger But Mainly Death Games, I wanted to tell y'all about some of the totally hip changes we've put in place!

"Some of you may have heard of something called a 'Cornucopia.' But am I the only one who thinks the word Cornucopia is so lame? What is this, a death tournament for *dads*? That's why we decided to ditch it! And we've replaced it with something totally awesome: the "TeenZone." Like the Cornucopia, the TeenZone is that hip spot-izzle for all your tournament-izzle needs-izzle—but with a fresh *teen* attitude!

We all peer around, trying to see what he's talking about. The only thing for miles is a fold-out table. It must be that. A disposable plastic tablecloth hangs over it. I guess they were trying to make it scary-looking, because it has a print of a cartoon Frankenstein on it. But he's carrying a heart-shaped box of chocolates in his outstretched arms towards a Bride of Frankenstein, and he's saying, "Will You Be My Valentine?" On one end of the table there's a tray of orange and purple Jello Jigglers shaped like ghosts, and on the other there's a bowl of Lays. In the middle, there's a karaoke machine.

"I bet you're pretty 'pumped out' for that new karaoke machine!" the announcer continues. "We used the money we would have spent on a death-announcing cannon to get it for you! We think you'll have a swag blast gettin' jiggy with it! And in the event that anyone in this tournament dies, a message will briefly scroll across its screen. We're sure you'll be using it so much that you won't miss a single announcement. A sign-up sheet is on the clipboard next to it."

Is there *anything* useful on that table? I'm actually having a hard time seeing. That's because right in front of Pita and me is an enormous bird that I probably should have mentioned before describing all that other scenery. The bird is eight feet tall with big buckteeth. A trail of feces follows its footprints and its two eyes look in opposite directions. A mockstrich! Just like the one on the pin the mayor's daughter gave me! This must be a good omen! It's also the perfect animal to serve as the symbol of a rebellion, I think for no apparent reason whatso—MWAHMWAHMWAHMWAH.

Without warning, the mockstrich launches into its trademark song. Uh-oh. Not good. Not only has it now gotten the attention of all the other sacrifices, the song it's singing sounds an awful lot like...

"Hey!" yells out one sacrifice. "Why are you guys late?"

And, as I'm about to respond and explain the whole boyfriend-girlfriend thing and how it's not true at all, the mockstrich starts up again,

MWAHMWAHMWAHMWAHMWAH.

"Oh man," yells out another sacrifice, "they were *kissing*! That's why they were late!"

AHAHAHAHAHAHAHAHAHAHAHAHAHAHAHAHAHAHA HAHAHA.

I try to tell them that no, we were not kissing, but it's no good. The other sacrifices are just laughing too hard. And it doesn't help that Pita is yelling out "Sorry, guys! We got carried away with the smooching!"

Finally, the laughter dies down.

"It's good to have moments of levity like this in a death tournament," says one sacrifice, wiping a tear from the corner of his eye.

"Okay, but back to that death tournament," says another, a sandy-haired, tall boy.

Everyone groans. "I know, it's a drag!" the boy continues. "But this is the day we've been training for. Now, the other team could arrive at any second, so gather round, and I'll lead us in a quick prayer."

Other team? I don't this guy has a very accurate conception of the Hunger But Mainly Death Games. But it's probably better for me not to point that out, since many of the sacrifices are already stepping forward to join hands in a prayer circle.

"Heavenly Father," he begins, as I creep towards the food table, "Please watch over us this afternoon, and, if it is Your will, please give us the strength triumph over the Watertown High Minutemen so we can move on to State." I spot an orange backpack lying on the ground, and snag it. Noticing that it has an unexpected heft, I unzip and find it's filled to the brim with freshly cooked meat. I shake my head in disgust. The Capitol's message is all too clear: we're nothing but "dead meat" in their eyes. And maybe something about the importance of protein. I toss everything out in disgust. Now, if

I can make it to the table and then the forest before these sacrifices realize—

"Um, attention, sacrifices. Attention," comes the voice of the announcer. "You're supposed to be killing each other. Just want to make sure that's clear."

The sandy-haired boy's jaw drops. Off to the side, a sacrifice who's been sipping a latte spits it out in shock.

"Wow..." the boy says, "This is so awkward...Crud...I mean, how do you guys even want to do this—GARGH!"

He's cut short by Scar, who has leaped behind him, pulled out his spine, wrapped it around his neck, and then stomped on his feet so hard that the pressure makes his head pop off and shoot into the sky.

"All right, rich kids! Let's roll!" he shouts, beckoning to the other careers. They start sprinting towards the table, and my only option is to leap out of the way. Looks like I'll have to put my hunting skills to the test in the arena, after all. While it's nice to have them, I had sort of been hoping to "reinvent" myself here. But I guess I can still tell people that my nickname back home is "Coolgirl Awesomegirl."

The other sacrifices can only watch as the big, bad careers take all the good stuff from the table. They take greedily take all the oysters, potato salad and milk and...and now that I think about it...they're taking foods that spoil really quickly, and a couple six packs of beer. "Have fun with all the yucky foods, *losers,*" says Glamorrhea as she turns her nose up at a table full of beef jerky and canned food items that will last for years.

With the careers gone, the rest of us are left to calmly apportion out the remaining food items. Oh wait, never mind.

Death tournament. Soon there's a huge dogpile of sacrifices stabbing and eating each other. One kid uses his severed arm as a club to cave another kid's skull in. One girl gets a grenade jammed into her throat, so she runs up to a boy sacrifice, latches on to his face, and starts making out with him so that his head explodes, too. Meanwhile, one boy is knocked down on top of a dead girl's body, only to discover that the girl is actually only paralyzed from the neck down—meaning she can still bite into his neck and sever his carotid artery. As he bleeds out, she drowns in the blood.

As I watch them maul each other, I can't help but note how convenient it is that all the kids whose names we don't know are getting killed at the very beginning of the Games. In fact, now that I think about it, it's *way* too convenient...

Two of the nameless sacrifices appear to realize the same thing, as they abruptly jump out of the dogpile and make a break for it. The first of them doesn't make it too far. Within seconds, a disemboweled boy from the pile throws his own intestines out as a lasso, and catches the boy around his waist, ripping his body in two. The second escapee, a girl, is luckier. She survives for a full ten seconds longer, before Capitol snipers quickly pinpoint the nameless escapee who is threatening to ruin the integrity of the Hunger But Mainly Death Games with a character we don't know the name of.

"I have a name!" she calls out. "I have a name and my name is—"

POW.

The top half of her head disappears, sparing us from having to remember more than like five or six names.

I look off into the distance, and hey, it's Mr. Sniper, from school!

"Best of luck in the tournament, Bratniss! All of us in Slum 12 are rootin' for ya!"

"Thanks, Mr. Sniper!" I say, as I turn away from him and I run right into Pita.

"My love!" he cries. "Thank the sweet angels I found you! Quickly, let's find some sort of kissing-cave! We'll be safe in there!"

I can't let this go on any longer. The Games have started, and there's no time for games, except the Games themselves. And that's when it hits me. The perfect plan. Because if Pita can say that we're dating…

"All right, Pita," I say. "I understand that we're dating." His eyes light up and he gasps in joy. I continue, "And now, since we're dating, I'm taking this opportunity to break up with you. It's over, Pita. You're dumped."

I gaze at him in satisfaction. In celebration of my newfound freedom to completely focus on the Games, I allow myself the luxury of ducking out of the way of a cloud of throwing knives.

But what Pita says next makes my heart stop.

"I understand completely, Bratniss," Pita says. "If you love something, then set it free."

"That's not why I'm breaking up with you! Which, I don't even need to do at all, since I never agreed to date you in the first place. I don't—"

"Hold on, I'm not done yet. So you set her free and if she comes back to you, after you've tracked her down using the homing beacon you inserted into her body, slipping the beacon piece by piece through her morning skunk milk over the course of ten or so years, then yes, you are allowed to kiss her forever."

Here I am, in the middle of the Games, and instead of killing someone I'm having to *break up* with someone I'm not even dating.

"Pita. You know that way you feel about me? I don't feel that way about you."

"You haven't said you don't love me yet.

"Okay, Pita, fine! Pita Malarkey, I do *not*—"

A booming guitar riff from the darkening sky cuts me off. I start to tell Pita I don't love him again but I'm cut off by more guitar riffs. It's a song from the Now That's What I Call Jock Jams #441 album: America John and the SpaceWolves present "The Star Spangled Banner."

Oh-hoooo say can you see, under the neon lights,
Big baby Jeeee-sus and his muscles,
Guns, apple pie, and then more guns,
For the la-hand of the free, and the home of the Year-Round McRib.

As the last chords of the song play, the announcer's voice booms out of the speakers, "Welcome to the Sprint Nextel University of Phoenix Touchdown Jenga Arena Sponsored by Red Bull®!" The sky turns into a scoreboard, because apparently they can do that with science now. On the scoreboard is a grid with the pictures and scribbled names of all the nameless sacrifices killed.

As I scan the list of dead kids, trying to make myself sad in that way you have to when someone from your school you don't know dies, I can't help but notice most of the dead sacrifices have pretty forgettable faces. I have to hand it to them: they cast this book pretty well.

There are a few exceptions, though. I see one girl dyed her hair pink, meaning she must have had some real spunk. I bet she—wait, no, that's just hair cancer. But here's one: a boy who did a goofy pic where he's holding up his glass eye! Or, wait, maybe the eye popped out and he's trying to catch it right as the picture is being taken. Either way, he's got this scream frozen on his face that looks really genuine and heartfelt. So, I decide to pay him the honor and respect he was so cruelly denied when he entered this godforsaken arena. I give him a name. It's a small gesture, but I hope he would have appreciated it. Goodbye, "Screamy."

Finally, I get to the bottom of the list, and there I see it: my name. Bratniss Everclean. Oh, no! I'm dead!

But then I look closer and realize I was looking at scribbles underneath the picture of some other generic looking brunette girl. Phew, that was close.

"And now," booms the intercom voice in a gravely, monster truck derby announcer way, "for your Sharkorade Sports Drink *Death. Of. The. Dayyyyyyy*!"

On the floating sky billboard, a video clip begins to play. It's Scar, wearing a Sharkorade jersey and helmet, using a sacrifice as a bat to kill another sacrifice, whose head shoots off like a baseball and tears the head off of another sacrifice in the distance. Somehow, the boy's body then explodes, and the video ends as a pre-recorded voice says, "Sharkorade. Kill your thirst—IN THE FACE."

The video ends and I'm left alone with Pita.

"I guess we're stuck together forever, huh?" he says.

I walk through the forest alone, still holding the block of wood I knocked Pita the hell out with.

Anyway, I'm lost in the forest now. Sorry for not going into further detail, but it's been a rough 72 hours. You know, you're more than welcome to chime in with *directions* or *advice*. You haven't been particularly helpful up to this point, reader.

But let's set aside our differences for now, because while I'm trying to hide in a big tree, I suddenly hear the sound of footsteps. The loud footsteps of someone walking either very clumsily, or deliberately loudly for ingenious trap-based reasons which I can only begin to speculate on. Somehow, I have a feeling it's the latter.

There's no time. I'd better hide in the bushes across from me. OW! Pricker bushes! Time to try these other ones! OW! Knife bushes! Mustering all the speed I can, I rush over to some barbed wire bushes. OW! Barbed wire bushes!

Not a moment after I've made it back to the safety of the Ebola tree, the shadow of the mystery competitor appears. And it looks like he or she is carrying a hideous trident. Either they're coming to kill me, or there's a bail of hay that needs to be moved around. But when the figure steps out into the clearing, I see that I'm mistaken.

"*Forkface,*" I whisper. Luckily, Forkface doesn't hear me, because she's too busy stuffing mud and sticks inside her ears. Huh. I guess she must be trying to suppress her sense of hearing, in order to develop some new, and more useful super-sense, like radioactive night vision? As if to confirm her, uh, keen intelligence, she heads over to a huge patch of poison ivy and begins to eat it by the fistful—a sure way to keep any cannibalistic sacrifices away from her. Yes, that Forkface is a wily one. I guess. This can only be part of an elaborate and...intelligent trap? Well, whatever, best to sit and wait it out.

By the time Forkface has stripped the area of all the poison ivy, poison sumac, and poison oak, and moved on, night has fallen. Through what little light remains, I look around me and confidently decide: I have no idea where the hell I am. I'd better walk to somewhere where I'm not so lost. But it's hard, because it's pitch black outside. I can't walk more than four or five feet without tripping and falling over. Would it kill them to put some lights out here, for those of us wearing heels?

It's also eerily silent. The only sounds are the crunch of leaves beneath my feet and my handbag's occasional pursefart. All signs point toward death—big, smelly old death. Yep, ignoring the fact that several chapters remain, all signs point to my death, at any moment.

Suddenly, I hear voices. It could only be one thing: sacrifices, coming to kill me. I need to think quickly. Fortunately, thinking quickly is one of my strengths, which is why I'm sure there's no way the huge, nest-like structure to my left harbors any wild or dangerous animals. I confidently walk inside.

Seconds after entering, I hear buzzing and, as I tiptoe through this structure's hexagonal, larvae-filled corridors, the sounds of liquid sloshing and mouths gulping. Finally, I turn a corner, and there I see them, gathered around a keg of beer. This is no normal, safe-insect hive, after all! This is a hive full of Buzzerguzzlers!

I'd better give you some background on hybridations before I get to Buzzerguzzlers, though. A hybridation is an animal genetically engineered by the military science department of the Capitol. Over the years, the Capitol scientists have succeeded in creating a few moderately dangerous hybridations, and a few others, like the Mockstrich, that were pretty much a waste of time. These include Panta Bears, which are ant-sized pandas; Grizzly Mares, these horses with really tangly manes; and Kangaropes, which are ropes that bounce up and down and keep their little rope joeys in a pouch.

But Buzzerguzzlers? They're actually dangerous: they're super alcoholic flies, whose bite releases alcohol into your bloodstream and makes you hallucinate and go crazy in that way that alcohol does. But that's not the end of it. If a Buzzerguzzler detects that you've consumed any alcohol in the last year, it will burrow inside your skin with its razor-sharp wing-claws and eat the surrounding flesh.

Outside, I can hear the group approaching the nest. Fortunately, I'm safe in here, because I've never had alcohol. So, I'll just wait things out. To pass the time, I'll use this nail polish remover I stole from Cinnabon as punishment for his terrible outfit, and get rid of Pita's little toe-job.

I pop open the top, and lower an eager nostril toward the lip. It gives my nose that refreshing, dry-erase board singe. As I'm working, I can't help but belt out my mother's old nail polish remover song.

"*Slather it on, slather it on*! *Take a shot and slather it on*!"

"Hey, Joe! You smell somethin' funny?" I hear a fly say in the heart of nest, between slurps of beer.

"Yeah." SLURP. "Smells like booze."

"Get outta he'ah."

What? What could the Buzzerguzzlers possibly be smelling? It's not like I have any alco—ah, crap, I'm stupid. Not only does nail polish remover have alcohol in it, I just took eleven shots of it.

"Nah, Mike, I swea'ah. Let's go check it out."

The slurping ends and the buzzing begins. The Buzzerguzzlers are coming for me.

I'm left with a terrible choice: death by fly, or death by teen. Sure, the flies will eat me, repurpose my skull for a fly funhouse of sorts, probably turn my eye into a snowglobe, keep the other eye just to have an eye around, hey, who knows, maybe even use my butt as a trampoline. But I wonder if it's the teens I should really fear. After all, flies don't tie a peer up with dirty underwear and circle the fat places of her body with marker. And they don't put plastic wrap over the toilet seat so that you choke when you try to get a drink of water between classes.

Again, you could make the argument that I'm not going to die right now. But it's not like there's a simple test where I can just look ahead and see if there are more chapters of my own book that I'm writing many years after surviving all of this. No, I need to make a decision *now*.

But as I'm taking several hours to exhaustively list the pros and cons of death-by-teen and death-by-fly, I hear it. A high-pitched shriek. "Help! I'm being held prisoner against my will! Come save me, beautiful ex-girlfriend Bratniss!"

It can't be. But I peek out and sure enough, there's Pita, hogtied in the grass. A wedgie reaches up from his butt, loops over his head and covers his eyes. Another wedgie runs around his hips and tucks into his neckline, all bib-like. A third wedgie reaches above him and loops over a tree branch, suspending him several feet in the air. A fourth, frontal wedgie loops over—okay, you get the idea.

Several feet away from Pita, the careers sit in a circle around Scar, who is drinking a can of beer and using a corpse's stomach like bongos. The other careers laugh uncomfortably.

Pita may be blinded by his underwear, but the second that stalker-nose of his picks up my scent, he'll start calling for me. I still have a shot at escaping, but I'm sure it will only make Pita think I'm trying to save him *again*.

Alright, flies, I think, resigned to death. *Come get your dinner*. I turn back toward the inner reaches of the nest, when suddenly the edge of the hive gives way. I try to scramble back up, toward the safety of the flies' mouths, but I'm falling, falling downward and—PLOP—I land right in the middle of the careers' circle and hit Glammorhea, who spills beer all over her face.

"Uh, hey guys."

It's like that moment that always happens when the weird kid from school walks into your party. You and your friends were just trying to hang out, but not anymore. *He* is here now. He asks you where the bathroom is. You point—my bathroom is over there—wait, no—don't go in there, weird kid. But it's too late. He's already in. He's doing his weird bathroom thing in there. There's no way he goes to the bathroom like the rest of us. His mark will be there forever. That wart on his hand is touching everything. You have to stop him. You pick up a butcher knife and start walking toward the bath—suddenly Stacey is all, "What do you think you're doing? He's just going to the *bathroom*." And she's reminded you of an important thing, you realize, making a note to kill her later, too.

So yeah, we all know how that goes. Isn't that just the worst, popular teen readers?

A beer-faced Glamorrhea thrusts a finger at me. "You're going to pay for ruining my makeup, bitc—"

BZZZZZZZZZZZ.

The Buzzerguzzlers are on her face in no time. Within seconds, it's just a hole for her skull to fall out of. Which it does. I can't believe it. I've killed her. I get the feeling that some small, tiny part of me wants to feel bad, but I smartly override it and start spraying beer on the rest of fleeing careers, hoping to get them Buzzerguzzled.

As I spray and spray, flecks of beer begin to coat my arms. Amidst the chaos, Pita squirms inside his maze of wedgies. "Hey, my buddies! What's going on? I hear flies!" But then his nostrils flare. I stop dead in my tracks. Oh shi—"Bratniss? Is that you, honeybaby?"

I take off after the careers. As I sprint, my legs begin to burn and my vision clouds. I've been running for almost eight full seconds. Weirdly, the careers ahead of me seem to be doing fine, almost as if they've had access to proper nutrition their entire lives.

Ten yards ahead, I can make out Scar. But I'm losing him, because he seems to be wearing some kind of super short high heels that don't even really have a heel—whatever you call *those*. I look down at my arms and legs and notice several Buzzerguzzlers have latched on to me. That doesn't matter, though. My hunting instinct has kicked in.

With every bit of strength I have left, I throw the beer can at him. I'm squinting, but from what I can tell, it's going to hit him right in the back of his head. He's going to get his stupid head eaten right off, LOL.

But then something not very LOL happens. He moves. And the beer looks like it's going to hit him lower. It…it seems that when you throw something at a moving object you have to take into account that the object is *moving*. That's weird. They don't teach you that in Girl Sports school.

The beer hits his butt, lamely spraying beer on his back pocket. So much for that—oh, no, wait, the flies are on him now. They're all over his butt, swarming and gnawing, really doing their butt thing.

"You will pay for my butt, Bratniss!" he yells in pain. "No one gets away with having my butt eaten off. *No one*!"

As he limps into the forest on his half-butt, my vision begins to fade. The Buzzerguzzlers are swarming my arms and legs now. My only hope is to find the thing Buzzerguzzlers hate most: water. But where do I find water? If I can't find it, then do I just produce it? But *how* do I produce water? Produce. That's it. I have to *produce* water. I hear a stream nearby, look down at the empty water jug in my hand, and realize what I must do: I have to pee on myself on national TV.

But this can't be any normal pee. I'm going to have to pee *all over* myself. No part of my body can be left untouched by my own pee. The Buzzerguzzlers will funnel through any spot I miss, and eat my insides out. This is going to be tricky.

I lie on my back and curl up into a pee ball. I must use every ounce of strength I have to overcome my innate revulsion. I must summon all the willpower I—oh, never mind, it's actually super easy (and fun) to pee on yourself. I can feel the Buzzerguzzlers lifting off, one-by-one.

And then, everything goes black. Because, embarrassingly, the warmth of my pee has me feeling sort of cozy, and I decide to climb up into a tree and take a nap.

When I come to, I'm in a daze. How long have I been out for? Long enough to have slept through the rest of the tournament, I hope. I look up at the huge hologram clock in the sky, as the minute hand ticks from 7:33 to 7:34. So: I've been unconscious for less than one minute. Dang it! Why can't I sleep through even *one* death tournament?

But now that I'm back, I can tell that I'm in a dire state. My energy levels have hit rock bottom. A dull headache pounds in between my ears. I'm having difficulty concentrating. And, more than anything, I have some sort of...*hungry* feeling in my stomach. What can it all mean?

Then, unbidden, an image from the past rushes into my mind. I see myself sitting on a chair in front of a table. In front of me, a piece of food rests on a plate. My hand reaches out and grasps that food, and then brings it up towards my head, after which my lips part and my jaw extends downward, creating an access point to a hollow area in which I place that food. And then, I see myself using the muscles of my jaw to move my teeth in such a way that they soften and tear that food into smaller bits, which I transfer down into my stomach with the help of my tongue and throat.

I'm utterly mystified.

And then I realize: I'm remembering myself eating. Humans need to eat to live. Sweet, merciful God, how did I forget that? I've always prided myself on having good common sense, and an inextinguishable will to survive. But this seems like a pretty fundamental mistake to me. What will I do next? Not set the alarm on my watch that reminds me not to light myself on fire?

So, I climb down from the tree and begin making some traps and snares. Of course, they're really easy to build and instantly work. As soon as I've turned my back, I hear the sound of a large animal being caught. And, from what I can hear, it sounds tasty.

"Shit," the animal yells. "SHIT." I lick my lips. A fire would be too great a risk now. No choice but to eat it alive, I guess. "Gotta get out of this trap," the animal says. It must have nicely developed vocal cords to be making these types of animal calls. Huge, delicious vocal cords, engorged with even more delicious being-eaten-alive-adrenaline. I grab hold of the net as the animal struggles inside.

"*It's okay,*" I whisper, bringing it up towards me. "*I'm going to make this as easy as possible—eyes first.*" I shove its head inside my mouth. Then, in that vibratey-ear-hearing way, I process it saying: "No, Bratniss! Don't eat me! I'm not an animal! I'm Roo!" I pull her wriggling body out, and to my surprise, she's right: she *is* Roo—that darling little sacrifice from Slum 11.

"What were you doing out here?" I ask. She blushes.

"I saw a pretty butterfly fly into the forest. It was so pretty to look at that I had to follow it! I'm sorry if I disturbed you here!" I'm taken aback. It might be the sweetest thing I've ever heard. And I heard it here, where misery and pain lurk behind every tree, underneath every rock.

"Oh, sweet Roo," I murmur, tousling her hair and straightening her outfit. As I do, a folded piece of paper falls out of her pocket. I pick it up and open it, ready for another dose of cuteness. What could it be? An invitation to her next tea party? A letter to one of her guinea pigs back home?

But it's a series of diagrams and maps...all of which seem to relate to me: "Route to Bratniss's tree;" "Areas on Bratniss's tree to release super-termites, to make her tree fall down in a way that her head is crushed;" "Spot to put C4 explosive putty in Bratniss's tree, to blow her sky-high once and for all."

"Uh, Roo? What are these?" I ask, reading yet another description that has "Bratniss" and "to Kingdom Come" side by side.

"I don't know!" she says, full of childlike wonder. "What *are* they? I saw them on the ground and I took them because I thought I could make some pretty paper dolls to sing and play with! What does that writing on them say, Bratniss? I'm too little and tiny to know how to read!"

"Are you certain you don't know what these say? I'm pretty sure this is your handwriting, because I can see that you're making another one right now," I say, pointing at a new diagram that she's furiously sketching. It's a drawing of my face labeled, 'Talks a lot...could easily throw a sword into her mouth.'

She blushes bright red. "They're all...silly jokes?"

I'm stunned. In the midst of all this horror, little Roo has found the strength to laugh. And in doing so, she has given me the strength to do the same.

"Got your nose!" I say. She giggles uncontrollably.

"Do that again!" she begs. "Do that again, but much slower, and expose your wrists so I can put this razor-blade bracelet on you!"

"Maybe later, sweetie-pie. Right now, we have to talk about some grownup-things," I say, ducking my head away from the joke-noose she's trying to lasso onto it, "Roo, will you be my ally?"

She's silent for a moment.

"You really want me for an ally? Even after I made those silly joke diagrams?"

"Sticks and stones may break my bones, but words will never hurt me, unless they're the living word-monsters the Capitol has created," I say, repeating an old Slum 12 adage. "Besides, I was a few seconds away from eating you. So maybe we can just…call it even?" I ask, extending my hand.

At that exact moment, the tree I was sleeping in explodes in a massive fireball. Roo grins nervously. "So...you were saying?"

"Um, what was I saying? Oh, yeah! Let's be allies."

We both know that it can't last forever. So, we come up with a thorough agreement. I pick up a piece of charred wood from the explosion and begin to write on the back of one of Roo's diagrams. When I'm finished, I present it to Roo:

"Bratniss and Roo are allies now. Signed, Bratniss and Roo."

"This seems really good!" she says. "I have a few suggestions, but maybe they aren't very important…"

"I'd love to hear them, Roo. I bet they'll be cute as a button, just like you!" I say, scooping her up and giving her raspberries on her tummy.

"That tickles!" she squeals. "Now, how does this sound?" I read her revisions out loud:

"'We, the undersigned, proclaim that from this moment forth, we are allied to one another.' Roo, that's very good! I bet you're gonna be a big, important lawyer when you grow up!"

She giggles. "Thanks. You didn't finish, though."

I read on:

"Due to the peculiar nature of the child-killing contest in which we are engaged—particularly its prohibition of a number of winners greater than one—we will each allow the other one instance of pretending to fall asleep, waiting till said party hears us snoring, creeping up on us, and then lifting a jagged rock above our heads, murmuring, 'Forgive me,' but right then the sound of an owl alighting from a branch wakes us, and we roll out of the way right in time."

"Huh." I say. "Yeah, I guess this is still okay, Roo. It's sensible, for sure."

"You're still not done."

"'The undersigned shall not be said to have reneged upon the agreement if her ally dies in a natural disaster, including, but not limited to: poison blow dart-shooting statue incidents; spiked walls slowly closing in on each other; or any of a particular set of wind patterns whose peculiar nature have been known to cause a plastic bag to engulf a human head and ziptie itself around the neck area, even if the survivor is suspected of having engineered the disaster for the express purpose of killing her ally, since the movements of the Earth are extraordinarily difficult to gauge.

'This alliance will only be severed if either party dies, if both parties agree to sever it, or if one of the parties realizes that her ally probably isn't on board with dying so that she herself can live.'"

I take a step back. "Hoo boy...I may have to think about this a little, Roo."

"If you don't sign the agreement, we can't play together," she coos. Some of the wording makes me nervous, but how can I not sign? After all, Roo sort of reminds me of my little sister, who means so much to me that she appears in maybe three entire paragraphs throughout the trilogy.

After that's taken care of, I tell Roo that our first act as allies should be finding some food.

"Have some of these berries," she says, holding out a handful of pitch-black deformed orbs that are oozing out a bubbling, neon green fluid that's sending waves of noxious gas into the air. "They're good!"

"Aren't those facemelt berries? I thought they were poisonous."

"Oh, you can totally eat around the poison! Like this." She turns so that I'm looking at her right side, and brings the berries up to her mouth with her left hand, swallowing them with big, theatrical bites. It doesn't seem like the most efficient way to eat. Nearly every time she does it, I see the berry fall out of her hand onto the ground, where it sizzles and flames.

"Mmm," she says, rubbing her belly.

"Thanks, baby Roo-ling. But to tell you the truth, I'm in the mood for something a little more substantial."

And I'm in luck, because we've stumbled across a mockstrich egg. I gasp. An egg: a symbol of hope restored and life renewed! Could it be some sort of sign that I'm destined to lead a nationwide uprising against the Capitol? Yes, I should have known that the mockstrich would be of the utmost importance to me, from the day I got my precious mockstrich pendant. I can't help but smile as I look down at the rainbow Silly Bandz I pawned it for. Damn, my arm looks cool.

By the time we've eaten our fill, dusk is beginning to fall. We put our heads together to try to decide what we're going to do about our competition. I consider our options. The careers must be furious about the Buzzerguzzlers. I don't think there's much to do except stay far, far away, and I tell Roo so. She frowns.

"That's not bad. But what if we were to...draw them towards us?"

"They'd kill us."

"Then I guess the only thing to do is to go to them."

"That would kill us, too."

"Right, right," she says. "So it's settled: you'll run straight into their camp, yelling and screaming, with no weapons and wearing mine-magnet shoes."

"I don't know, Roo. It's getting pretty late."

"Well, if we're done for the day, what do you say we have a sleepover?"

"Sleepover?" I ask, surprised. I've never had one before. "Those weren't allowed back in Slum 12. At least, that's what the popular girls in my grade told me."

"Then let's have one tonight! They're super fun! You stay up talking, pig out on snacks, and then you tie this rope around your neck and see who can jump down hardest from the tree! Come on! We can practice now, if you want!"

Roo leads me to the place where all this fun "sleepover" business is going down: a pitch-black cave that has the unmistakable smell of rotting sacrifice bodies. Roo assures me that it's only rock B.O., so I follow in after her, as she lights the way with a dead lightning bug she got from a sponsor.

"Roo, I think I just stepped on a skeleton," I say, directing the bug's single ray of light towards it.

"Nah, that's a stalactite."

"Okay, but there's definitely a head resting on a pile of intestines next to it."

"Stalagmite," she replies. A few minutes later, she stops. "We're here. This is where I was staying before we became allies."

"It's really nice. But did I just step in a massive pile of bear poop?" Roo doesn't seem to hear me.

She yawns. "I think it's about time to turn in." But a question is tugging at me. I decide to ask her. I must.

"Roo," I say, "why did you keep trying to kill me today?"

She gasps. "You noticed?"

"Yeah," I whisper. "It was pretty obvious, actually"

"Then why did you stay with me?"

"I like you. And, more importantly, you're too tiny and precious to be harmful." I pause. Why not admit it? "And part of me was hoping that eventually we could transform your murderous energy into niceness, and we could be like those hippo-with-a-bird symbiotic relationships where you hopped around inside my mouth and cleaned my teeth."

Roo stares at the ground, and then looks up at me with a pained expression.

"I guess I have some things to explain to you. You know I'm from Slum 11, right? The Human Experimentation slum?"

"Yeah. But to be honest, I've never understood what that means."

"It means that they experiment on us."

"What's experimenting?"

"You know, that thing people do in science?"

"What's science?"

Roo looks at me in disbelief. "You mean you never had to take People-stretchology or Intro-to-Sewingheadstogether in school?"

I shake my head. Roo pauses to think.

"I guess the easiest way to explain it is that in Slum 11, our basketball teams are really fun to watch, because our players are twenty feet tall and can jump thousands of feet in the air, but most mornings we wake up on operating tables with weird bruises and no idea how we got there. That's what science is."

I give one of those 'shut-up-no-they-didn't' faces, even though this sounds like a pretty even trade-off.

"Did they experiment on you?" I ask. Roo nods.

"They wanted to make me an unstoppable killing machine. But they weren't finished when I got chosen for the Games. Now I have the insatiable desire to kill, but not the ability."

"And what about the other boy from your Slum? Bear? What did they do to him?"

"I don't know," Roo replie. "He never talked about it. All he wants to do is spend his time alone, down by the river, catching salmon in his mouth." That poor soul. The experiments must have been pretty grim, then. I wonder if it has anything to do with why he looks like a bear.

"I appreciate you sharing this with me, Roo. And that you've decided to stop trying to kill me."

There's an awkward silence.

"I haven't. I brought you in here so Bear could eat you. I've done it a few other times."

She shines the dying lightning bug over to one corner. There are the corpses of the feral twins from Slum 8—one in a pile of Bear's poop, the other in a puddle of his pee.

"Dang it, Roo."

But Roo doesn't answer.

"I said *dang it*, Roo."

Still no answer. I look over at her. She stares at me with wide eyes. Sticking out of the middle of her chest is the razor sharp tip of an arrow. She sinks to her knees. "Hug me, Bratniss," she says, "Line the arrow up with your heart and hug me."

And just like that, she's gone. Whoever did this is going to pay. I look up and see Dylancobra standing at the mouth of the cave, reloading his bow and arrow.

"You murdered her!" I yell. "How could you!"

"It was easy enough," he replies. "Do you think that only your *precious Scar* is powerful enough to kill someone?"

"What? What are you talking about?"

"I'm sick of being a sidekick, damnit!"

"Dylancobra. Take a deep breath, okay?" I say, trying to calm him down. "Now, does Scar know you're out here? You remember about the buddy system, right?"

"Oh, I remember it, all right," he says with a hollow laugh. "How could I forget? All my life, I've been trained to be a sidekick. When I was little, they would tie me down in front of a TV and make me watch hours of footage of Robin and Scottie Pippen! They made me practice getting second place. *Practice* it! I had to learn how to lean away from the tape at the end of races. How to leap in front of the basketball hoop at just the right moment, so that I'm the guy who gets the dunker's nuts in my face. Do you know what that does to a kid? Well, it doesn't matter. Because with every kill I get, I'm one step closer to not being a sidekick. I'm sorry I have to do this to you, Bratniss, but there's no other way."

"You're wrong, Dylancobra! The key to not being a sidekick is in your heart! You're a perfectly good and scary sacrifice on your own, you just need to accept that!"

"Huh," he says, letting the bow drop to his side. "I guess you're right. Okay, then," he continues, swinging the bow back up. "I guess this is just to win the Games, then."

Damnit!

Just then, I hear a twig snap. I spin around. Bear!

"Thank God you're here. Bear!" I cry out. "Dylancobra just murdered Roo!"

Dylancobra sneers, his arrow still cocked. "That's right. And I suggest you stay where you are, unless you want to end up like your puny friend."

Bear considers him for a moment, and then continues lumbering forward. I guess he's grieving so deeply that he no longer wants to live. And Dylancobra is more than happy to oblige him.

"You should have listened to me!" he shouts, letting an arrow fly. It lodges in Bear's shoulder, but he doesn't seem to notice, and starts eating some raspberries from a bush. Raspberries, the grim fruit of the mourning.

"That's right, let the arrow, uh, kill you slowly," Dylancobra says uncertainly, loading up another. Just then, we hear the loudspeaker switch on.

"Attention, sacrifices," comes the voice in the sky. "Due to an oversight, it seems that we have accidentally selected a bear instead of a boy for one of the slum's sacrifices."

All three of us gasp, except Bear, who's scratching his back against a tree.

"We're going to do all we can to get the situation under control," the announcer continues, "But until then: for the love of God, avoid the sacrifice you've been calling, let me see, here…"

We listen intently.

"Here it is," he says. "'Bear.' Thank you."

All three of us scream, except for Bear, who does more of a roar, grabs Dylancobra in his jaws, and carries him off into the forest.

I return to Roo, and the tears begin to fall. She looks so precious, lying there. And that's when I realize: it's almost as if…as if this is a scene from a movie. A beautiful, heartrending scene in a movie. The kind of scene that teaches us about dignity and compassion and love, and the indomitable human spirit.

It's too beautiful not to start singing a haunting song:

Oh, hey, everybody, don't you think this would be,
A lovely scene, in a popular movie?
Sit back, relax, enjoy the show,
And doesn't Roo's death make you want Coke?

Here is a scene, so moving and gorgeous,
That the Teen Choice Awards, whatever those are, will surely take notice.
If you're kids making out, can you please stop?
First of all, this isn't romantic, and second of all I can see you from inside the screen and it's gross to watch.

I end my song, but the violinbirds (a hybridation I forgot to tell you about before) continue to play—mournfully, but in a way that is also very dramatic, while the arena's set designer carefully arranges a bed of flowers for Roo.

There's nothing left for me to do here, I realize, except flush Roo down the toilet.

I gently carry her body over to the nearest restroom, and fling open the door.

Inside, the temperature is oddly stifling, and everything is covered in an orange glow. I peek down into the bowl and see why: whoever used this last must have eaten a *ton* of lava. That is, unless this stuff in the toilet is…actual lava. But if this stuff is really lava, then how come my finger I just put in the toilet hasn't—oh, wait, yep, half the finger is missing ohmygodohmygod THIS IS HOT LAVA!!!

Sure enough, just as I notice the lava, it notices me, in that way dangerous forces of nature do in dramatized accounts. The lava oozes out of the toilet, edging closer and closer to my Hello Dead Kitty socks. "C'mere, yummy girl," it bubbles in sleazy Lavanese.

This burial is hardly going as planned. Yes, I want to flush Roo, but I want to do it respectfully, with proper toilet water. Not with the filthy melted contents of the Earth's core. But the only other toilet is miles away, thanks to the cruelty of the Gamemakers.

That's when I realize: this is exactly what the Gamemakers want. They *want* us to turn on each other. They *want* us to throw our friends into lava!

"*Well, what are ya gonna do*?" I think, as I toss her into the bowl and get the heck out of there.

From outside, I hear her screaming stop almost instantly—replaced with snaps, crackles and pops. Either her body is burning quickly or there's a fresh bowl of Rice Krispies and milk in there and her body is just burning normally. I'm not entirely sure why she was screaming though. Dead people do the weirdest things sometimes.

I turn away from the door of the port-a-potty behind me, and almost trip over a cardboard package. I pick it up to inspect it. Stamped on it is the silhouette of a man swinging a snake like a baseball bat against a metal fence, as a chorus of skunks cheers him on, and a bird flies in the sky. This is Slum 11's official emblem, and it represents the harmony of man and skunk through mutual hatred of the snake, and also birds exist. It's nice, but Slum 12's official emblem of a man stuffing his mouth with poop is more regal.

But why is District 11 sending Roo a package right now? This is ridiculous. How does Slum 11 not know that the proper way to contact a dead person is by writing on their Facebook wall?

But maybe I'm getting this wrong. Maybe this package isn't for Roo. Maybe it's for someone else—someone who was close to Roo, but is still alive, and is in this tournament, and judging by the pink bow and name sticker on this box is a girl named Br...Bra...

Like I have time to sounds things out right now. I'm stumped. And I can't possibly bring myself to open someone else's package. "That would just be crazy," I whisper to my knife, Betsy, who totally agrees. But just as I'm about throw my hands up in the air, all *I-give-up*-like, I realize: hey, Bratniss you dummy, this isn't a gift for Roo. This is a gift for you! The people of Slum 11 must have seen how good friends you and Roo were for the like 15 minutes that you knew each other and now of course they want to spend millions and billions of dollars they don't have in order to send you a *gift*!

I untie the bow and I can hardly believe what I see: a freshly baked slice of poisoncake! How thoughtful of those sickly, disgusting little Slum 11 people! I lift the poisoncake to my nose and take in its earthy, outdoorsy, bathroomy scent. Almost instantly, the insides of my nostrils start burning and I go blind in one eye. I think I've lost control of my bowels but I can't check.

Ooh, I can tell this cake is gonna be *rich*.

Slum 11's kindness astounds me. These people have somehow found the time to make me this delicious slice of cake and...and that's when I see that they've really outdone themselves, because beneath the poisoncake is a *second* gift! It's a timer with various, colored wires running into it. Its digital timer is counting down and the entire thing smells like gunpowder.

They've given me a *watch*—a watch that I can use to tell the time! As soon as I learn my numbers! I can't imagine what they had to go through to make me poisoncake *and* a watch or even what possibly could have motivated them.

Although I have to admit, there's something peculiar about the packaging. The name is also kind of weird too. Poisoncake. Hmm, poison...*cake*. There's just something suspicious about that word... "cake"...and...and now that I think about it, the watch is bizarre, too. It's a little, well, *big*. Plus there are all those wires. And the watch batteries being two sticks of dynamite is a peculiar choice as well.

Then I realize: whoa, check yourself, Bratniss. A week in the Capitol, and you're already starting to judge gifts. What's next? Turning your nose up at a steamed licedog? "Too spicy for me, Mr. Grilled Lice Sausage Vendor." Come on, Bratniss, don't forget your roots. These are wonderful presents from wonderful, stinky people.

But this isn't just a gift. This is a showing of unity. It shows that Slum 11 and I are in this together now. We are the 99%, or something. This new feeling of community as well as the feeling of the poisoncake burning through my hand brings tears to my eyes. I open my mouth to sink my teeth into the yummy treat when BOOM.

Everything goes black.

When I finally come to, I'm disoriented and confused. How long was I out for? Did I just do that thing where I pass out in order to skip ahead to the next big scene?

Please, not another instance of me passing out for the cheap effect of drama. There's no way. There's just no way a writer would have a main character do this so many times. Not unless...it happened in separate books...so readers wouldn't catch on to the trick.

But enough of playing with the fourth wall for now, because I then realize there's a voice over the intercom, announcing something.

"Attention, remaining sacrifices and bear. Please make note of the following, super-special rule change. This year, there will be *zero* winners of the Hunger But Mainly Death Games.

The words echo through my head. No! They can't do this! They've given all of us a death sentence! I've played along with their little Games so far. I've done everything they wanted! Now, I have no choice but to take a stand! And nothing will teach them a lesson like me killing myself.

"Huh? what's that, Bill?" the announcer whispers, *"Two? What do you mean TWO SACRIFICES? Then why does it say ZERO on my CUE CARD, you IDIOT!*

That's when the spanks start.

SPANK. "*You like that, Billy boy? Huh? You gonna fudge the numbers again?*" SPANK. "*Go ahead, fudge 'em! This hand loves it some intern butt! Take 'em! Take the spanks!*"

Finally, the announcer clears his throat. "My apologies for the mix-up, everyone. Okay, here we go: this year, the last *two* remaining sacrifices will be crowned champions of the Hunger But Mainly Death Games. So, yes, two sacrifices can win this year. Two of you can live. The rest have to die."

That's not so bad, I guess. At least it's not as if you have to be in a relationship with your partner in order to—

"Oh, gosh, sorry, folks, I almost forgot. To take advantage of the rule change, the two winning sacrifices have to be dating. We thought it would be a neat way to gives these Games that cool *teen* spin we talked about earlier."

These Games are getting weirder and weirder by the second.

"Oh and we replaced the toilet water with lava thanks so much bye."

I shouldn't be surprised. It's not the first time the tournament has had a rule change. One year, there was Bring Your Dad to the Tournament Day, which ended in a ton of awkward "my dad can beat up your dad" type stand-offs. Then there was the time they announced, "All the air is now poison air!" before quickly having to restart the tournament with 24 new sacrifices. And who can forget the year the tournament was played "Baseball Style," where you could only kill someone if you were wearing a hat?

But those were stupid *little* things: dads, hats, killing every single sacrifice in a matter of seconds, etc. Now the adults have gone and changed the number of winners and added a weird romance angle.

Well, it's probably best that I lay low, keep hydrated, and give myself some time to sort this all out.

But first, yelling for Pita. "PITA! PITA PITA PITA PITA PITA!" I yell, emptying my water bottle on the ground.

I have to tell him that, even now, we're not going to date. No crazy new stunt of his will change this fact. For me, it's a purely pragmatic decision. I'm one of three girls left for the remaining three boys, and Pita is the weakest of all of them. We've had a weird history, Pita and I, but I still think I should explain my decision to him. I bet he'll be pretty reasonable about it.

So, I continue calling out. But no matter how long I call, or how loudly and joyfully I play my steel drum, he doesn't come. There's not even a single catcall from within the forest. What's wrong with him? He invades my privacy night and day, for weeks on end, but the second I need him around to preemptively break up with him, he's nowhere to be found.

But I'm wasting time. Maybe it's more important for me to go out and find the person I *do* want to date. I'll have to head to the careers' encampment.

As I make my way there, I run over the possibilities. Forkface, Emily, and I are the only three girls left, and Pita, Scar, and P'rank are the only three boys. Emily has been in with Scar and P'rank since the beginning, so it's probably too much to hope that she isn't with one of them. That leaves Forkface.

For some reason, I'm not too worried about her. Because I'm beginning to wonder if Forkface might not be as smart as everyone seems to think. Like, if she's so smart, why does she keep getting stuck in that trap I built for hedgehogs? All the hedgehogs have been able to avoid it.

And why is she always running toward things that are on fire, and rolling into things that are made of fire?

And why is she constantly eating dirt? I just don't see the tactical advantage of anything she does.

Some part of me suspects that "take fork out, put fork in" song of hers doesn't have even any other lyrics. I hope I'm not alone here, but I don't think it's a very good song.

So, yeah, I'm not too worried that she'll have gotten to Scar and P'rank before me. I guess the only thing to worry about now is whether the one who isn't taken will be *willing* to date me. All they know about me is that that I tried to painfully murder them a day ago.

And here I am, right at the clearing where their encampment is. God, I love books. From the edge of the forest, I can tell the two of them are engrossed in some kind of argument, but I can't quite make out what they're saying. I creep closer.

"That whoopee cushion system you set up better protect our food supply, P'rank," Scar is saying. "If anything happens to my ice cream, I'll kill you."

I look behind him, and see mounds of rotting food surrounded by a perimeter of inflated whoopee cushions tied together with a string. The deviled eggs seem to be doing particularly badly, and something is writhing around inside the yogurt. P'rank goes over and stirs it.

"Your ice cream will be fine," P'rank replies. "See, I'm moving everything up to the top of the heap, closer to the sun's preserving rays. Anyway, don't we have more important things to worry about now? You heard the announcement."

So, they're already going to start fighting over which of them will get the privilege of dating me!

"Yeah, man," Scar says, solemnly, "I'm a monstrous, scary dude, but even I feel sorta weird about, you know...*going* on the ground."

"I don't think you have much choice," P'rank says, "Use one of those lava-toilets and you'll burn up like a moth in a flame."

Wait, what? This should be the least of their worries! I mean, the fact that they're even mentioning it, it's almost as if...*they're already taken*. But that can't be!

"At least it's the only problem we have to deal with right now. You've got Emily, and I've got Glam. Really gotta thank my sponsors for sending in a team of doctors to bring my lady back to life," says Scar.

But I saw her skull fall out of her head! And if Glamorrhea is somehow still alive, and dating Scar, this means everyone but Pita is taken! I should have known that even here, even in the face of death, the popular kids would still manage to date only each other.

And that's when Glamorrhea walks into the clearing. I can't believe what I see: her head is literally just a skull with some blond hair. Even so, she's still blathering on about herself. "I wonder who's going to play me in the movie they make of this. Who's that actress who was hideously disfigured in a car crash? Because that one can play you, Emily."

Emily nods sadly.

"Sup bitches," says Scar.

Glamorrhea laughs. "Oh, Scar, you're so very sweet. Now, won't you be a dear and accompany me to the loo?"

"What the hell are you talking about? The toilets are full of lava now, remember? Go behind a tree, or something."

"Preposterous! I'd rather die!" Glamorrhea says, raising her voice. "Aiming our poop into a bowl and then funneling it into a big tank of poop underground is the only thing that separates man from beast. Now, Scar, stick your hands out and receive my lady-droppings!"

"*Whoa*!" says Scar, "I don't know if we've reached that stage, yet!"

Across from them, P'rank is trying to get to know Emily. "Emily," he says, "Do you...like pranks?"

"Pranks? You mean, like, walking slightly behind someone at all times? So you can be ready to brush her skull-hair?"

"No, I mean, like, making someone think there's a fart? Or any other butt gas,"

"Ah! Like jumping in front of your friend and claiming her fart as your own!"

P'rank shakes his head wistfully. I feel for them. As lower-level popular kids, they're stuck with each other, even though they don't have much in common. You might even say that it's one of life's greatest tragedies.

Nobody's paying attention right now, I can steal their supplies! All that rotten food looks pretty grisly, but there's got to be something in there that could be useful.

Just then, I feel something brush past my legs. I look down and stifle a yelp as a badger waddles past me and into the clearing. It's headed straight for the food mound.

"There's no need to fear, Scar, my butt-treacle is as skinny and elegant as my figure," Glam is saying.

"Hey, look!" shouts P'rank. "It's Bratniss!"

Oh, no! They've spotted me! Wait, no, they're pointing at the badger.

"Are you sure that's her?" Scar asks.

"It's *obviously* her," says Glam, "I'd know that hobo haircut of hers anywhere."

"Where's her loser boyfriend, then?"

"Are you kidding? That cave we dumped him in might as well have been a tomb."

"Whatever, I'm still not convinced it's—"

At that moment, the badger reaches the perimeter, triggering the first whoopee cushion. A loud fart rings out.

"Okay, that's definitely her," says Scar. "You know what they say: 'If it looks like a badger and farts like a badger, it's Bratniss.'"

"And she's farting on our food!"

"Kill her!"

Frightened by the commotion, the badger snatches a slice of green pizza, and scurries back towards the forest.

"Do something, Scar!" yells P'rank. "She's trying to escape to her farting den! We can't get in there! It's filled with too many poisonous Bratniss farts!" But Scar isn't looking at the badger. He's looking at the mound of food.

I follow Scar's eyes to the tipped over container and the puddle on the ground.

"My ice cream," he says, twitching involuntarily. "It's...gone."

He turns to face P'rank. "You promised me. You promised me that you could make an impenetrable wall out of rubber bags filled with air."

"I didn't say that! I said they would alert us in a funny way if someone got close!"

Scar steps toward P'rank and...SNAP.

He steps on a twig.

Then, SNAP.

Scar snaps his "Killing Time" slap bracelet onto his wrist.

SNAP.

He has paused for a moment to eat some fresh sugar snap peas.

SNAP.

Ahh, washing them down with a refreshing Snapple. The bottle cap teaches him an interesting fact.

SNAP.

"Scar, dearest?" Glam calls out, picking a few snap-dragons, which she probably means to wipe with. "Are you going to snap his neck or not? I hope you haven't forgotten the condition I'm in."

"Okay, fine."

SNAP SNAP SNAP.

Scar starts snapping his fingers in that "scary" way the gangs in West Side Story do.

Then SNAP!

Scar chomps down on a ginger snap before punching cleanly through P'ranks face.

"Oh, thank goodness," Glam says, "Now, open up your hand that isn't covered in brains, so I can deposit my womanly tushy-berries."

"Glam! Either go on the ground or hold it in!"

"That's easy for you to say!" shouts Emily. "Ever since Bratniss had your butt eaten off by flies, you've had a constant stream of poop running down your legs!"

"Shut up, Emily," Scar and Glam say in unison.

"Now, as I was trying to say before I was so *rudely* interrupted," Glam continues, "That's easy enough for you to say. Ever since your behind was eaten off by those nasty little flies, you've had a constant stream of poop running down your legs. You're a man, and it's fine if you act like a barbarian. But I am a lady. Come now, Emily. We're off to the washroom."

Emily runs after her.

"What are you idiots doing?" says Scar, "Emily, get back here. Girls don't always have to go the bathroom together. You know you're committing suicide, right?"

Emily looks back at him, through misty eyes. "And if I let her go alone, and she ran into a stall-dragon, then it would be *murder.*"

And with that, Glam flings open the stall door. She and Emily step inside, and both girls comfortably go to the bathroom together.

I'm kidding. They are killed instantly, by the lava.

Somehow, Glam's burning skeleton manages a few final words.

"Farewell, ugly people. Oh, and Scar, I'm breaking up with you for not letting me poop in your hands. Wanker."

Even though these people mistook me for a farting badger, I can barely hold back my tears. No one deserves this. This must be so difficult for Scar. I can't begin to imagine what it's like to see that happen to your girlfriend and her sidekick, and to have been helpless to stop it. He looks up into the sky, visibly pained, and shouts, "YES! I'M SINGLE! I'M SINGLE AGAIN! Nothing can stop me from pooping any and everywhere!"

He hops around and begins beating his chest and yelling, like one of those crazy humans we gorillas keep in the zoo. (I mentioned earlier that we're all gorillas, right?)

"And, now that I'm free, I can spend every waking hour hunting down that disgusting badger-girl who messed up my ice cream. And when I find her, I'm going to torture her to death." He smiles happily.

Hey, maybe Pita isn't so terrible after all. He's creepy, but in a relatively harmless way. And, my God, at least he won't try to kill me! Besides, it's not as if the Gamemakers said I had to fall deeply in love with him and have a perfect relationship.

So. I guess it's finally time to make Pita my boyfriend.

The rain pours down outside the cave as I crouch over Pita. (Luckily, he was in the first cave I spotted.)

"Come here to kiss me a lot, darling?" he asks weakly. "I...heard the announcement." Ah, Pita. Always on, even when you're lying in a pool of mud, gravely injured. I'll have to learn to tune it out, though, since my life depends on dating him. But I've got to make him understand that it's going to be on my terms. Those terms being that our relationship lasts for the duration of this tournament and not a moment longer, and that said relationship will *not* be kissy.

"How's my leg?" he asks. "Am I still going to...have the moves like Jagger?"

"Before I answer that stupid question, let's make a few things clear," I say. But right before I start explaining how it's going to go, I glance down. What I see fills me with dread. Either Pita is covering his leg in a blanket of pulled pork, or he's in serious trouble.

Well, even so, I still need to lay down the law about this relationship business.

But I never get the chance, because suddenly, the announcer's voice rings throughout the arena.

"Greetings, remaining sacrifices! I'd like to give you some wonderful news. You're going home! All the parents in the country banded together and decided this tournament was too cruel. Of course, I'm only kidding. Now, please watch this footage we've secretly taken of your families learning how to be happy again."

I peek out of the cave and crane my head upward. One by one, images of our mothers, fathers, and siblings returning to normalcy crawl across the sky.

There's Pita's dad, unscrewing Pita's mom to reach her mainframe, and removing the black mourning chip that robots use to feel sadness.

There's Scar's family, going to District 4 to chase some people with big lawnmowers.

There's Forkface's little brother, helping his mom tinker with their homemade "Automatic Tablesetter XL77," and the mom giving him this look like, "You know what? I have a feeling it's going to work this time."

And, finally, there's my mother and Pig. Mom's tending to her new boyfriend, a gigantic cinnamon roll, and then accusing him of cheating, and then murdering him, and then Pigrose smiling as she has a nice Sunday breakfast for once.

I let out a little gasp. My heart sinks. Seeing them and not being able to talk to them makes me feel like a ghost, only without all the fun haunting and making people go crazy powers. The announcer continues. "However, I do have a *little* bit of good news. We're throwing you a special party by the TeenZone. There, you will each find something that you need dearly. Oh, and don't feel the need to take a *bath* before you come…Because there's going to be *plenty* of a certain *red liquid* to *bathe in* once you get here…and when I say 'here,' I mean the Murderbloodsuperkillbath Party. MUAHAHAHAHAHAHAHA!"

Pita and I look at each other for a few moments. Then he turns away and closes his eyes.

"I think I'll take a little nap," he says. "A nice, little nap."

"Uh…are you sure don't you want to discuss this murderbloodsuperkillbath thing?"

"What's to discuss?" he says. "I'll see you when you get back."

"The thing is, I'm sort of not sure if I should go at all," I reply. "I mean, all that evil laughter at the end. It made it sound as if they're planning something dangerous. And you know how our sponsors only give us the absolute crappiest things."

Pita whips around, his eyes filled with panic.

"Please, Bratniss," he says, grasping my hand and looking up at me beseechingly, "You have to go. There might be medicine for me there. The kind of medicine that heals a shredded leg."

"Does that actually exist, Pita?"

"Yeah, it does! It does! If only I could remember the name! Legicillin? DoctorProfessorWizard Justin Bieber's Magic Leg De-Mangling Serum? Whatever it is, I know that it exists, and is not a figment of my going-into-shock imagination."

Before I can answer him, we hear a knock on the cave door.

"Package!" a voice calls out. "Package for Bratniss Everclean, from her sponsors."

I sigh, and then make my way out into the light. The deliveryman is holding an envelope for me.

"Hey, how's it going?" I say, scribbling my signature for him. "What is it this time? Some dust clumps to use as body armor? A strand of hair to use as a sword?"

"Hey, I could ask the same about you and my Christmas bonus," he says. I give a short courtesy laugh, but then I look up and see how pissed he is. "Do you know how dangerous it is for me to be bringing you crap out here?" he asks.

I give a shrug and head back in. "Hey, there's your problem. Stop bringing me crap," I say, as a giant fireball smashes into his back. Inside I tear open the envelope and pull out a piece of paper. "*Go get the medicine,*" it reads. "*It's your only chance to save him...and yourself.*"

"*And*?" I wonder.

"*And remember that if he dies, you die,*" the paper says/it doesn't actually *say* that, I hadn't finished reading the whole thing.

I sigh. "I guess I am going to go, Pita." But he doesn't reply—he's already fast asleep, having a Power Rangers dream.

"Rangers! As you know, I'm your leader and the best fighter," he murmurs, "But I think I'll sit this one out, so I can observe your skills and teach you how to improve." Then, a moment later, in a whisper: "*Phew*. I'm glad I didn't tell them the real reason I don't want to go fight, which is that I'm too scared."

When I approach the TeenZone, there isn't anyone in sight. Perhaps I've made it here before the others. I strain my eyes to see what they've got waiting for me on the fold-out table. And there, next to the dusty karaoke machine, crouches the medicine. Huh. Awfully tall and human-like for a bottle of leg-medicine.

That hulking figure can only be Scar. I guess this is it. Please use the remaining blank pages to write your own end to my sad tale, or to write a note of condolence to me. Or, better yet, to make into a money-holding envelope that you put lots of money in and then send to:

Aaron Geary and John Bailey Owen, Scholars, Men of Letters, and Distinguished Authors
- of -
The Hunger But Mainly Death Games: A Parody
Prisoner #330192 & Prisoner #49051
Rikers Island
Cellbock E-7

Maybe include some guns, the kinds of guns that would be strong enough to blow up an entire prison wall. Thank you!

I walk closer to the figure. "All right, Scar," I manage. "Let's see what you've got." I shove him and, oh my God, he just topples over. I...I must have superhuman strength, because there's no way Scar is that weak. I stand over his crumpled body and, right before I stomp down on his head to finish him off, I say to him, "Hope this doesn't leave a *scar.*"

His head folds in half and I realize that I've been fighting a Sharkorade life-size cardboard cutout of Scar. They must have propped it up in the TeenZone as a cool decoration.

"BRATNISS," a metallic voice rings out in the sky. "YOUR TIME HAS COME."

I look up to see a fighter jet bearing down on me, its machine-guns blazing. I leap out of the way, and watch as the pilot ejects, sending his jet hurtling into a nearby mountain. His parachute deploys, and he begins hurtling downs toward me. Scar! I rush to the table and grab the medicine, but he's already on the ground, sprinting at me. He's just too fast. Right as I'm about to reach the woods, he lays out and grabs hold of my ankle, pulling me down to the ground.

It's all over, I think.

And then, a man emerges from the bushes. It's a Gamemaker. He must be here to revel in my death, the sick freak.

But to my surprise, he pulls a whistle out of his pocket and blows on it.

"Kids? Kids?" he calls out. "Sorry, I'm gonna have to call a little 'timeout' here. I'm not trying to interfere, but one of our bear sensors around here was tripped, and we don't want to take any chances. So just hold up for a second while we look around, and—"

At that moment, Bear emerges from the woods behind us.

The Gamemaker freezes.

"Do *not* go near that bear!" he hollers at us. "Back away slowly! No sudden movements! You hear me? Back away from the bear! Oh, but feel free to go near that pit of spikes over there."

That's when his cellphone lights up.

"Ah, crap, I think this is my boss. I've got to take this, okay? Just hold on! Hello?"

A shrill voice emanates from the receiver, loud enough for us to hear.

"Yeah, hi. This is *Scar's mom*. I'm watching from home and I'd really love to know *what the hell you think you're doing.*"

"Uh, excuse me?" asks the Gamemaker.

"You know exactly what I'm talking about, bub! I'm talking about putting a *bear* in the arena!"

The Gamemaker tenses up.

"Yeah, that's right!" Scar's mom continues. "A *bear* in the arena! Do you really expect a child to be able to kill a *bear*? Killing some pasty-faced starvation victim is one thing. Killing a *bear* is another! You're liable here! You know that, don't you? Oh, you're liable out the ass! Putting a child in harm's way! It boggles the mind!"

The Gamemaker looks at me in a silent plea for help. I shrug my shoulders apologetically.

"HELLO? ARE YOU LISTENING TO ME!" she screams.

"I'm here, ma'am. We're working hard to getting this situation under control as I speak, but you're gonna have to let me put you on hold for a sec, so I can—"

"HOLD? What, so you can go to the *bear store* and buy another *bear* to throw on top of my son? I don't think so! You're going to tell me exactly how you plan to make this right!"

He pulls a weighted net out of a box and starts fumbling around with it, trying to untangle it so he can use it on Bear. "Ma'am, I'm trying to make things right as we speak," he says. "I understand your concern, but I assure you, we're on top of it."

"I want to speak to whoever's in charge immediately. And it clearly isn't you! So run along and go get your boss!"

"Ah, well, see, right now he's sort of busy setting up this radioactive waste trap thing that the kids are going to walk into later this afternoon, so—"

"This *afternoon*? No way is that gonna fly. Scar is going to be at soccer practice."

The Gamemaker's face drops, and he begins to stammer.

"Do you mean to tell me..." Scar's mom begins, slowly and pointedly, before bursting into a shriek, "THAT THERE HASN'T BEEN ANY SPORTS PRACTICE HERE AT ALL? AND HOW DO YOU THINK MY SON IS GOING TO MAKE THE U-17 TRAVEL TEAM WITHOUT *PRACTICING*?"

The Gamemaker looks ill. "Listen, we've been doing our best with the resources we have. Your son has been getting all kinds of exercise here. There's lots of fighting and scrambling around, and, you know, another thing is, he's got to win this entire thing to even be able to go back to soccer—"

"And you think he's not going to win? Look at him! He's a cyborg-warrior-demon, of course he's going to win! Take a look at the title page of this book if you don't believe me. It says *By Scar*, doesn't it? Idiot! You're an utter moron idiot! And to think, you work with *children!*"

At that moment, we all hear a rustling, and Forkface emerges from the woods, holding her stomach and moaning.

"What is that?" Scar's mom asks. "What is that!"

Forkface stumbles forward, her skin bright red and neck oddly swollen. She reaches the Gamemaker's feet, and then drops down to her knees. Her mouth is smeared with something.

"Take fork out...put fork in...that's how me me Forkface..*win.*" and crumples into a heap, dead.

The Gamesmaker looks down in horror, and a pries a food wrapper out of her hands.

"Oh, my God," he whispers, beginning to read it. "'*This product was manufactured in a facility that also processes peanuts.*'" He shakes his head. "Makes sense, that the only person who could beat her...was herself."

"YOU'RE LETTING THE CHILDREN IN THIS ARENA COME INTO CONTACT WITH PEANUTS OR PEANUT PRODUCTS?" Scar's mom screams from the phone.

"MA! Shut the hell up!" shouts Scar. "You're knocking me out of the zone."

"Scar? Is that you? Scar!" she calls out. "Come over here!" Scar rolls his eyes, but trudges over.

"*Yes*, Ma?" he asks sullenly.

"Scar, I want you to kill this man! Right now! Painfully!"

"MA! I'm busy!"

"Very well, Scar! But don't be surprised if I let your little brother play with your Playstation!"

"UGH, FINE," says Scar, pressing a button that turns his rocket launcher arm into a razor sharp egg-beater, which he proceeds to push through the Gamemaker's face. "But keep Jeremy away from my videogames!" he says, as the man falls into a heap on the ground. "Those are frikkin' mine! I got them because I got stars on *my* star chart! And if you're going to let Jeremy play with them even though he didn't read *nearly* as many *stupid books* as me, then why do we even have a star chart, mom? MA? MA!!!"

"Sorry, lovey, I'm on the freeway right now, and I can see some 'Peace'keeper cars up ahead. Don't want to get a ticket for talking on my cellie. I love you, Scar. Now go kill that disgusting Crapshit, or whatever her name is. Mwah!" The line goes dead, and Scar turns toward me.

"You're going down. All the way down to Dead-person Town."

"Not so fast," comes a voice from behind me. I whip around. To my astonishment, it's *Bear.* He lumbers up and stands in front of me.

"If you want the girl, you'll have to go through me first."

"*How are you talking?*" I whisper to him.

"*I'm not talking,*" he whispers back. "*This is all in your head.*"

Scar laughs maniacally.

"You think this *bear* can stand up to my heatseeker missiles? That's the stupidest thing I've ever heard."

Bear curls his lip, revealing a set of razor-sharp teeth. "*Let's see how you like my karate.*"

"Wait, wait, wait. You know *karate*?" I say. "Come on."

"*No time to explain, Bratniss,*" Bear says. "*You need to get to safety.*"

I run all the way back to the cave. And, damnit, forgot the medicine.

I run back and grab the medicine from the table, then head straight back to the cave. "I got the medicine, Pita," I say. "And you were right. Somehow, it's going to be able to piece your leg back together. All you need to do is take it twice a day."

"Thanks, Bratniss! I owe you! But are you sure that's *all* I have to do? There aren't any *other* directions are there?"

"Well, no, I—"

And then I see that he's right. The directions continue on the other side.

I slowly rotate the bottle. "Medicine must be taken twice a day...and administered under the guise of a full-fledged, loving relationship."

I feel lightheaded. How can this be?

Then, in a flash, it hits me: this is a novel for young adults. Think about it: as a young adult reader, you must run into books that talk about "the power of love" all the time. Like, the main character suddenly realizes, "Oh, the only way to defeat that evil monster and save the world is through *love*." And you're sitting there going, "No, it isn't! What the hell are you talking about! The way to save the world is to do something cool and unexpected and satisfying! For the love of God, there's a nuclear missile bazooka sitting right next to you!"

And that must be the explanation for why Pita's medicine requires a loving relationship to work.

Ha, ha, listen to me, making fun of "the power of love," and then resorting to it myself as an explanation. The vicious cycle continues, I guess. Maybe you'll break out of it one day when you write your own book. Good for you.

When I look up from the bottle, I see Pita's beaming face. He looks...handsomer, I try to tell myself. "What were those extra directions, Bratniss?"

I have to do it. I know that. I have to be a nice, comforting girlfriend to Pita. Do everything he wants me to. Make him my life. Talk about a terrible message, but what choice do I have?

The message I got from the sponsor was all too clear that if Pita dies, I die. I take a deep breath.

"Don't you worry about that, dear...I have something I want to ask you. Pita, will you be my boyfriend?"

Pita reacts the way I assume most boys do when they are asked by a girl to be in a relationship. He flaps his hands around all Oprah-like and politely shrieks yes, again and again. And with that, and his high Rockette-kicking around the cave, my fate is sealed.

I've never had a relationship before, so it's all new to me. There are phone calls. *Long* ones. Even though we don't have any phones and live one foot away from each other, he insists that talking on the phone is one of the most important parts of a relationship. So, we do it for several hours, every day.

"Brrring-brrrring!" he goes, "Brrrrring-brrrring!" Then I have to 'pick up' and act excited to hear his voice. He has us talk about our days first, which, in his case, means narrating out every thought and every movement he's had, right up until, "And now, I'm talking to you. And now I'm still talking to you. I'm having so much fun talking to you because I love you so, unbelievably much."

Talking about how much we love each other: that's the second half of the conversation. You have to come up with things you love the other person more than, and you're not allowed to repeat items. "I love you more than...afternoons with grandma and grandpa," he'll say. I'll reply, "I love you more than...uh...uh," and when he fills in the blank for me—generally something along the lines of "all the stars in the sky" or "any boy in the world"—and he'll do it with this downright unbearable 'Oh, you're learning' wink. Did I mention that he makes us do phone shapes with our fingers the entire time?

After that, it's time for an endless handholding session. An hour of clockwise stroking, followed by an hour of counterclockwise. Fifteen minute break to de-sweatify, then five more sets. The de-sweatifying period does little good. Our cave is so small and tight that the sweat never fully evaporates away, instead condensing into tiny clouds that sprinkle us with tiny drops.

"Isn't it romantic, holding hands in the rain?" Pita asks.

There are also the pointless fights, which, according to Pita, are another necessary part of any relationship. Maybe it's that I forgot our nineteen and a half-day anniversary. Maybe I didn't compliment him enough on the new shape he's pushed his increasingly oily mass of hair into. The only consistent thing about our fights is that there's always another one around the corner.

After a hunt one afternoon, I come back into the cave and he whips around and glares at me.

"Hello, Bratniss," he says icily.

"Uh...hi?" I respond.

"I KNOW YOU WERE FLIRTING WITH THAT ROCK!" he screams.

And, every day, the kissing. Pages and pages of it. ("Page," by the way, is a length of time that we use in Pandumb. It's equal to "roughly one billions years.") The amount of kissing I have to absorb is hard enough. What's worse is that Pita is disastrously bad at it. I'll admit it: I hadn't kissed all that many guys before this. I've never had a boyfriend, and the first time I played spin the bottle, I accidentally spun too hard and the bottle flew into this kid's neck and shattered. That sort of put me off kissing for a while.

Even so, I get the feeling that Pita is one of the worst kissers in history. Like, when we first started doing it, he was under the impression that kissing mainly involved the teeth, and mainly pressing your teeth against the other person's and slowly rubbing them back and forth. It took a long time before he'd instinctively put his lips against mine, and there are still a lot of times when he shrieks, "Eww, slugs crawling over each other! Back to teeth-on-teeth! Back to teeth-on-teeth!"

And all of it—all of it—is unbearably boring. The days roll by, all of them the same. For a while, I hold out hope that something interesting will happen again. But, eventually, the grim truth begins to dawn on me: there will be no relief from this boredom. The Gamemakers have either forgotten about us, or decided they've seen a lot of kids die already, so why not see some kids get driven insane by boredom?

I watch the seasons pass. The leaves fall, and a chill sets in. The mockstriches begin their long walk north, to an even colder place, because they are stupid. How long have we been here? No way of knowing. Days blend into weeks and months. We kiss and we kiss but nothing more, because, luckily, Pita still doesn't exactly know where babies come from.

Winter arrives. Our breath is visible inside the cave. Not because of the temperature, but because we haven't brushed our teeth in so unbelievably long. I hope that it will slow down Pita's kiss-drive, but he pays as little attention to our breath as he does our hideously chapped lips, or my scruffy beard.

One day, Pita turns to me. "I feel like I haven't seen you in forever, you know?"

"We spend every second of every day together, Pita. What could you possibly mean?"

"Yeah, but sometimes you're off in the shadows and I can't really see you, and it makes me worried that you're hiding in there on purpose because you've stopped loving me!"

"Pita, this cave is one big shadow."

"I know, and it's tearing us apart!" he hollers. "I'm sorry I said that, Bratniss. I love you so much. So, so much. Let's go out to a nice dinner tonight. You know, on the other side of the cave, the one where there's not so much bat poop. And you can catch some kind of delicious animal and cook it, and use the fat to make some candles, and, I don't know, maybe make a table from a tree you chop down? Thanks, sweetheart."

"Pita, are you not the least bit tired of sitting in this cave?"

He looks nervous and starts wringing his hands. "Oh my God, oh my God, I hope this doesn't mean we're going to get divorced after our kids go to college. Do you think it means that? Do you think this is a relationship where the love won't last? DO YOU?"

Before I can respond, the loudspeaker booms out: "WILL YOU PLEASE *DO* SOMETHING! ANYTHING! YOU'VE BEEN SITTING AROUND FOR *MONTHS*."

"Hey, it's not our job to make this exciting!" I yell back. "*We* don't like the Games! We think they suck!"

"Okay, kid, I guess *I'm* the one who's wrong. Me, the Gamemaker, who's been doing this since you were in electric shock-diapers."

"Believe me, I don't mean this to be insulting, but I'm pretty sure that you *are* the one who's wrong, here."

He sighs derisively. "I'm going to look in the Hunger But Mainly Death Games rule book, but only to humor you."

There's a long silence.

"Ah, shit, I'm not finding anything about entertainment responsibilities in here. Tell you what. Come down to the fun party we're throwing at the TeenZone, and we'll call it even."

"No way!" I say, "The last time it was a horrible trap!"

"This time it's not, I promise! DJ Evilmonsters will be spinning the swankest new jams...at the Happyfungoodnicedance Party! "

"We're not going!" I scream.

"Does DJ Evilmonsters have Nelly?" asks Pita. "I bet he has Nelly!"

"If you're not going to willingly walk into this trap—*party*, I mean party—then I guess I'll have to force you to go. You do realize that we have control of the entire arena. You're not going to like what happens to people who disobey us…" his voice trails off as we hear hands shuffling around on a keyboard.

"Ah *ha!* HERE!"

There is the groan of a lever being pulled. Far off in the distance, we see an anvil drop from the sky into some pines.

"Nope, nope. Okay, hold on. How about…THIS one!"

The click of a switch, followed by a beep. A laser shoots through the sky and roasts a flock of violinbirds, even further than the pines.

"Damnit! Why didn't anybody label these controls!"

And now, the sounds of hands clattering on a keyboard, pressing as many keys as possible. In the distance a plane firebombs a wheat field. Elsewhere, a cow with grenades in its mouth floating down in a parachute. A silo full of acid tumbles gently down a hill. Man, this guy really has no idea what he's—oh, damn—now the cave is on fire!

"There! Got it!" the announcer yells triumphantly.

"We've got to run!" Pita screams, shooting up to his feet as the pulled pork falls off his lap and the bottle of ketchup he was using for blood falls out of his pocket.

"Pita, your leg…it's…"

"I said RUN!"

We move as swiftly as our TeenZone pogo sticks will take us. The fusillade of deadly items continues—poisonous cannonballs and vats of piping hot chili and snakes with saws dangerously taped to their heads and, well, it all kind of makes me wonder, isn't this kind of wasteful? All of this, just to kill a couple of kids?

"Hurry Bratniss!" Pita says. "There's no time to think about whether or not this is kind of wasteful. All of this, just to kill a couple of kids."

And he's right. This internal debate can probably wait until after I've ducked that cannon-launched exploding baboon—OOHOOHOOHOO—that just sailed over my head. It's good to know though that at least Pita is thinking similarly. No, not similarly, but the exact same. Word for word. Wait a second.

I stop running. "Pita, how did you know I was thinking that stuff?"

"No time to talk! We're in mortal danger! Watch out! A deadly gust of wind!" he says, whooshing air with his hand.

“I thought something, and then you said it out loud, verbatim, immediately after I thought it.”

“Who knows what those dastardly Gamemakers will think of next! There’s no time to ask questions! Good heavens, an incendiary grenade! Take cover!” he yells, making explosion sounds with his mouth.

“Pita Malarkey, if I run my hand through my hair and find a mind-reader chip, I am going to kill you.”

He pauses.

“Come on,” he laughs nervously, as he reaches over and begins vigorously combing his fingers through my scalp. “Do you have any idea how *crazy* you sound right now?”

I duck out of Pita’s grip and roll backwards between his legs, simultaneously ripping the earpiece out of his ear, ninja-style, or whatever style means gymnastics, and picking at ears.

“What are you doing? And where are you going with my earpiece that doesn’t tell me everything you think?”

Great. Just great. I have a microchip stuck somewhere on my scalp, and its broadcasting my thoughts to the world. “Pita Malarkey greatly annoys me.” “I kind of need to pee.” “Maybe I should try to avoid dying.” Ugh, now everyone is going to know my secrets!

There’s got to be some way of deactivating it. After all, it’s just a stupid little piece of electronics. Although wouldn’t water have deactivated it by now? Then I remember: the last time I showered was the day of the Reaming. I know, I know, kind of gross. In theory, at least. In practice, I’ve hardly noticed it. Sure, there’s that greenish trail of smog that follows me everywhere, and lately when I hunt I’ve discovered I can just walk over to an animal and it'll fall over dead, nowhere near my trap.

An old van falls filled with lead bars falls and crushes a tree nearby, which reminds me: I should be running. I've got to get to safety. My life depends on it, and I also want to get to the bottom of whatever crap Pita is trying to pull.

I turn to Pita. "Where to?"

"That party the nice man was talking about! Where else? I hear they have a limbo pole."

"Are you stupid? The last 'party' almost got me killed!"

But it's too late. We've arrived at the TeenZone.

I guess this is it. I get down on my knees and open my arms to the sky. I'm ready for it. Ready for the afterlife. I'm sick and tired of this death tournament and even sicker and tireder of Pita Malarkey. Come and take me, Death.

"Bratniss, what are you doing?"

I open my eyes. Pita stands in an empty clearing. Other than some scraps of rotten food and some loose eyeballs and ears, the TeenZone is vacant.

"See? Not a trap at all," he says. "We're early. You go do your make-up. I'll go gather some paper that we can fold into pointy party hats."

But just then, Scar bursts through the trees, running right toward us. And he's wearing this awesome Che Guevara shirt that is a slightly different color from the ones you usually see. On top of that, his hat is on backwards and the hologram sticker is still on because that stupid fashion thing endured the apocalypse as well. Which all begs the question: where does he get these awesome sponsors?

"Run!" he screams. "Run for your lives!"

On top of that, he also has brand new shoes. Air Force Childkillers, I think they're called.

"CAN YOU NOT HEAR ME I SAID RUN! RUN!"

And did I mention he's wearing sunglasses? They're all black and shiny, like cool sunglasses should be.

He's slowed to a light jog now, "Listen to me, I'm serious! There are horrible monsters coming. There, right behind me. I am literally pointing at them."

Yeah, mm hmm, I *might* look over your shoulder and let my guard down so that you can finish me off. Real original, Scar, I think as I begin pelting him with anything I can find—pebbles, a fistful of grass, a dead kid's shoe with the severed foot still in it.

"Ow! Stop it! At least let me run if you're not going to listen to me!"

I've got Scar by the collar and am about to thump him over the head real good with a bubble gum wrapper when Pita grabs my shoulder, "Bratniss, he's right. Look."

Alright, fine. I begrudgingly peek over his shoulder. Hmm, so there are some monsters. And I guess they *are* pretty terrible. There's that white froth spilling out of their helmet and all down the front of their black armor. Maybe Scar is right. Maybe those are some weird townies trying to crash our party. I mean, monsters, monsters. Scar and I take off running.

But Pita doesn't. Instead, he just stands there. What is he thinking?

"Come on, Pita!" I yell.

"You go on," he calls out, "I'm staying."

"So you can what? *Fight* them? Pita, you don't know how to fight! Remember all those times you thought you were headbutting the bullies in their fists and making them hurt so much they laughed? You weren't winning!"

"Look, I've made a fool of myself here. The following you everywhere, the making you my girlfriend on national television, the slipping love potion in your drinks at every meal..."

"What was that about the love potion?"

"I owe you this much. Someone's got to slow those monsters down. And I...I want you to live a long and happy life, and to take long rides across windswept beaches as a musclebound man in a flowing white shirt holds the horse's reins in his strong hands, like on the covers of those beautiful books at the grocery store."

So, this is seriously happening. Pita Malarkey is giving his life so that I may go on living. I'm not sure what to do. No boy has ever done something like this for me before. Come to think of it, no one has ever really done anything nice for me. How is it again that people reciprocate kindness? What are the words? There are, like two or three words you're supposed to say. Quick, Bratniss, THINK!"

"Pita, thank...uh...umm..." but my words are failing me. And the monsters are almost on us."

I give Pita once last, grateful look, and turn away. From over my shoulder I hear him say, "Oh, and when you see her, tell my mom I love her."

With that he takes off, straight for the horde of armored monsters.

At the edge of the woods, I collapse. My lungs are searing, but the pain serves as a reminder: I'm still alive.

"I can't believe what Pita did," I whisper. "It was so incredibly brave."

"It was actually pretty stupid, I think," Scar responds.

Of course, Scar doesn't understand. How could I ever expect him to? He was raised to win, not to love. It doesn't matter what Scar thinks. Pita didn't die as a boy; he died as a man—a man still eagerly waiting for the onset of puberty, but a man nonetheless.

I can't help but sneer at the cowardly Scar.

"So...uh..." he begins, awkwardly.

"What? What do you want?"

"We should probably start acting like boyfriend and girlfriend so that the tournament can be over."

The thought hadn't even registered. Scar and I are the final two sacrifices—I hear a loud roar in the distance. Okay, the final two non-bear sacrifices. All I have to do is agree to be his girlfriend, and I can go home to the Crack, where Greta, that small baby-girl, and that big murderous woman are waiting for me. It doesn't sound great, but at least I'll have that year's supply of hot dogs that all Games winners get.

But is that what I really want? To say 'yes, Scar I'll wear your girlfriend ankle shackle,' and just pack up my belongings and go? Becoming his girlfriend would be a slap in the face of Pita's legacy, and I'd probably end up like that girl in that sequel to the movie "Ghost," where the ghost boyfriend decides he actually *isn't* cool with his ex dating another guy and comes back and spooks everyone to death.

"And to be clear," Scar continues, "We don't need to stay together after the tournament, or anything. This is simply so both of us can survive."

"Cut the crap. I've seen you out here. I've seen what you do. You'll probably kill me with some fancy gadget the second you get the chance."

"No, I won't. I understand why you're scared of me, but I don't want to kill you. I want the killing to stop. I've lost so much in this competition. My butt, for one. And my ice cream." He gives me a pointed look.

"The ice cream was an actual badger."

"Shh, shh. There's no need to blame defenseless animals. And there's no need to put up an act, anymore. I know what it's like. Because when I killed all those people, that's what I was doing: acting. I thought it was my best chance to win. That's how they expect you to act when you're from Slum 1. I just played it up. Hell, this isn't a rocket launcher," he says, pointing to his arm. "It's a melon baller."

"Yeah, okay." I deadpan, skeptically.

"Seriously! Look!" he says, pressing a button. A long, silver melon fires out of his arm and explodes an abandoned car nearby.

"Anyway, you heard what my mom was like. Every hour of my life has been planned. First soccer practice, then choking classes, and then killing people with a violin bow lessons."

It's then that I realize for the very first time: Scar is a human being. He's a victim, too. He's not the enemy. Adults are.

"So, Bratniss Everclean," he says, getting down on one knee, "will you be my Hunger But Mainly Death Games girlfrien—"

But before Scar can finish, a monster flies from out of nowhere and tackles him to the ground. Scar does his best to fend off the monster's advances, but the monster is too strong. It pins Scar down and, despite Scar's best efforts, slowly lowers its breadknife toward his throat. I try my best to pull the monster off of him, but it's just too strong. With a few whirs and clicks, its head suddenly turns around a full one hundred and eighty degrees and examines me. "Target: Bratniss Everclean. 16 years of age," it says robotically, "Objective: Make girlfriend. Course of Action: Resume killing of target called Scar."

Wow, there's something fishy about this monster. And a breadknife? Why on earth does it have a breadknife?

I sense something behind me. Another monster! I whip around to cave its head in with a plastic Solo cup. But it isn't a monster. It's Pita.

"Pita! Help Scar!"

"Oh, looks like I missed one of the monsters," he says. "And one of the really dangerous ones too. Whoops." He sits down and yawns.

"Make it stop! Help!" yells Scar.

But it's too late. The monster manages to stab Scar just before Scar rips off its head. The monster's severed head rolls over and settles at my feet. The helmet pops off and I see...it's bread. The monster is made out of bread. The froth I saw was just icing.

"I've been killed by...bread, Scar says weakly, in a way that conveniently lets us know he is dying.

With what strength he has left he grabs me by the collar, "Promise you won't tell anyone. Promise!"

"No one will ever know," I say, nodding my head into the cameras.

Scar's eyes roll back in his head, all dead-like, and Pita jumps up excitedly.

"I did it!" he says, rushing over and hugging me. But I suddenly realize that he's covered in flour...that crusts stuck to his shoes...he's even *still kneading some dough.*

"Pita," I say slowly. "Why in God's name do you have that rolling pin?"

He gives me a chilling stare. "Look on the bright side, Bratniss. At least this means there actually *is* a party."

"One, two, one two," says a man standing behind a set of turntables, "That's what DJ Evilmonster was tryin' to tell y'all. But now that you're done with all dat monster mash, it's time to party down with some monster jams!"

"No!" I yell, "DJ Evilmonster, don't you dare touch those wheels of steel! In fact, just get out of here."

A record scratches loudly as Evilmonster pauses and shrugs. "Aight, y'all, it's about that time. This is DJ Evilmonster, signin' off. Remember, I do bar mitzvahs, weddings, pool parties, anything you can put a beat to and get people shakin' them butts." He unplugs his system, grabs his turntable, and walks into the awaiting firing squad.

"You!" I say, thrusting a finger in Pita's face, "You were behind the monsters!"

Pita laughs, "Please, Bratniss, give me a little more credit than that. You really think it was just the bread monsters? What about the Reaming? What are the odds that the two of us would get picked? But here we are, Bratniss. Dating. After all these years, we're finally dating."

"Wait, wait, wait. You rigged the Reaming? Then why did you put yourself in the girls—"

"So I got pranked a little! By those mean old cool boys. Who cares, I wasn't about to let it ruin everything. So I had to improvise a little...turn on the waterworks to make you feel embarrassed. You took the bait." he says, raising an eyebrow oh-so-evilly.

"Oh my God. You mean..."

"That's right. There is no Mr. Bear."

My jaw drops.

"And from the moment we got on the train to the Capitol, everything else went exactly according to plan. My perfect, flawless plan."

"Pita, this is sick! How can you—wait, getting captured by the careers was part of the plan?"

"A MISTAKE! One *minor* mistake. But it ended up being a lucky one, because when you heard me screaming for help, you realized you couldn't bear to see me hurt, and wouldn't be able to go on living if you didn't rescue me right then and there." When you came to my rescue, it was the first time you felt a real bond with me. Not yet love, but closer, closer."

"No, Pita, that's not what happened at all."

"Oh, what does it matter! It all worked out in the end, didn't it?"

"I *guess*. Do you really want me to be happy that we survived the death tournament you threw us into unnecessarily? Like, I guess the way you used that fake diary entry to eventually inspire the Gamemakers to change the rules was smart, but we could have died at any point before then."

"Uh, yes, yes. Thank you. That diary was...it took quite a bit of planning."

"Pita, are you trying to tell me something?"

"Okay, I messed that part up, too! I had to sneak into the Gamemakers' hut and plant the rule change because they didn't bite on that diary entry! I'm sorry, okay! But here we are, we both survived! We're both winners, and it's all because of me, and now we can date each other in peace!"

Just then, the loudspeaker pipes up, "Excuse me, remaining Hunger But Mainly Death Games sacrifices. It's been brought to our attention, by you, because you just admitted it in front of us, that one of you broke into our hut and forged an announcement saying that there would be *two* winners.

"Now that we know it was fake, I regret to inform you that we're not going to abide by it. Only one winner this year, same as every year. Gosh, I don't even know why I'm apologizing. Just get it over with okay? Feel free to use these Red Bull® Negotiation Wands courtesy of Red Bull®," he says, referring to the shiny axes floating down to us on parachutes. "Oh, and don't even think about committing suicide with those facemelt berries you keep eyeing. If you did that, we would obviously kill your families in retaliation."

Pita and I look at each other. "All right, Pita," I say. "You're the one who brought all of this on us. But we both know that I'm stronger, right?" He nods, and I continue, "So how do you want to do this? It's your choice."

"Cardiac arrest brought on by the most strenuous making out ever, please," he says solemnly.

"Fair enough," I say, picking up the axe.

But as I lift it above my head, everything around us begins to rumble. Off in the distance, I can see explosions, and they're coming closer. *It's not enough*, I think. *Even doing exactly what they want isn't enough! They're going to kill us both anyway! Ah, well, I brought this axe all the way up here. No sense in letting that energy go to waste.*

I hear the sound of feet rushing up towards me, as I'm taking my third "practice swing." Better get it over with, and land this one right between Pita's—

"Bratniss, stop!" a voice calls out from behind.

I whip around, and I can't believe what I'm seeing. It's Greta! And he's wearing body armor and carrying a huge shotgun! And there's a massive army of people following him. Could this be? Could Greta finally have a real role in this book, instead of basically being the character equivalent of scenery?

"Greta!" I cry out, rushing up and throwing my arms around him. "What are you doing? And how did you get here? Who are all of these people?"

"Shh, shh. All in good time, Brat. Now, you know that old saying we have back in Slum 12? 'You should never be the first person to test the flying-suit you made by taping about a bajillion pairs of dragonfly wings onto an old shirt'? Well, I was thinking that we could head over to Bonebreak's Bluff now, and give this new dragonfly suit I made a try. It's really safe, I promise."

"Erm, excuse me, that's not actually why we're here," says a striking, middle-aged man woman, who walks up to me and extends her hand. "We brought Greta along because he had some homemade nuclear warheads we wanted to use." She tousles Greta's hair and hands him a fistful of earthworms. "Go and play, Greta. Bratniss and I are going to talk. I'm Sacagawea Coin, by the way. It's so very nice to meet you."

"But we don't have time to talk!" I protest. "Whoever you are, you've all put yourselves in great danger! 'Peace'keepers will be here any second!"

"No, Bratniss, they won't," Coin says. "We've destroyed the Capitol, once and for all."

"That's impossible!"

"Not with social networking," she replies with a mischievous smile. "It was pretty easy, especially after Facebook and Twitter added those 'Execute Dictator' buttons a few months ago. Greta's weapons of mass destruction were also quite helpful."

"But why?" I ask. Can this really be happening?

"Because ever since we started watching you in the Hunger But Mainly Death Games, we were goners. You're a star, Bratniss! And we're your biggest fans."

"You're our hero!" a young boy calls out. "You taught me that I could have my bully's butt eaten off by flies!"

"And you taught *me* that I could have my *own* butt eaten off by flies!" says a deeper voice, even further back. "It cured me from my bullying ways!"

"And that there's no shame in going to the bathroom in the woods, or in the yard! Whenever you need to go, it's best to do it wherever you are at that very moment, inside or out!" says a third.

"You taught me it's okay to fart all over everything while stealing ice cream!"

"I can't thank you enough," I say, my heart overflowing with gratitude. I can't believe it. This nightmare is finally over. "Are any of you from Slum 12? Where are my mother and Prim?

"Don't worry, they're doing well," says Coin. "They wanted to come, but, you know, bus fare being what it is these days. We'll get you back to them as soon as possible. Before we start that journey, though, we're wondering if we could ask you for one favor."

"Anything," I say, my heart overflowing with gratitude. These people have saved me. Whatever they ask, I will do. I *must* do.

"Okay, great, great!" she replies. "Here's the situation. As we've said, all of us are huge fans. But inside the group as a whole, we're actually sort of split down the middle into two subgroups: one that thinks you should date Pita, and one that thinks you should date Greta. Call them Team Pita and Team Greta, I guess, but it's not too important."

"Uh-*huh*," I say, and looking out over the crowd, I can see that they're sort of standing in two distinct clusters. I have a feeling the one on the right is Team Greta, because there are fewer of them, but they seem to be a lot more dangerous and insane-looking. I'm beginning to realize where this might be going.

"So, before we leave, we want you to choose one of them to date! And then, of course, to eventually marry and have kids with. Sound good?" Coin asks.

"I don't know how to put this..." I begin, "But not really."

Horrified gasps sweep through the crowd.

"What do you mean?" the woman shouts in horror. Before I can answer, we're all distracted by the sound of a man making his way through the crowd.

"Hey, hi, 'scuse me," he says, as he squeezes by people. "Sorry I'm late, everybody! Pardon me, pardon me. Wow, totally overslept! Call me crazy, but I wonder if we might actually miss our evil dystopian government. Hard to be late for an early appointment when you're woken up by painful shocks at four in the morning everyday. Ha, I'm only kidding!"

Finally, he makes it to the front of the crowd, only feet away from me.

"Carry on, little girl!" he says merrily, and then turns to the teenager next to him and says, in a low voice, "Now, which one of these guys is Jacob, and which is Edward?"

A swell of aggravated groans rises.

"Are you a complete moron?" replies the teenager. "You're thinking of contestants from The Hunger But Mainly Boring Vampire Games. That was, like, a decade ago."

The man smacks his forehead with his palm. "Ah, you're right, you're right. *Brain fart much*? Okay, carry on!"

"What I'm trying to say," I begin, breaking it to them as gently as possible, "Is that I don't really think it's *necessary* for me to choose right now. The circumstances are too insane! And besides, you definitely don't need to find the person you're going to marry when you're a teenager!"

Some of the people in the crowd begin to nod their heads as if what I'm saying is reaching them.

"Sorry to interrupt again," says that man. "This may be a stupid question, but if you don't find the person you're going to marry in high school, how do you ever expect to have a vampire-baby that almost kills you?"

"Oh, come on!" comes an aggravated voice from the back. "You've got to be kidding me!"

A woman whacks the man on the back of the head with a stick. "Twi-hards die hard!" she shouts.

"Argh!" the man says, clutching the area that was hit, but doing his best to stay chipper. "I hear ya, folks, I hear ya! Say no more, my mistake!" He pauses, wiping away some blood. "Keep going, girl-character from *The Night Circus*."

"All right, that's the end of you," says a huge biker, going up to the man and snapping his neck. "Now that that's out of the way, continue teaching us a valuable lesson, Bratniss!"

"I think that's it," I say. "That's all there is to it. I'm not ready to choose someone to date now. Does that make sense?"

"Yes!" says a woman wearing a shirt that says 'Team Greta,' "I think I speak for all of us when I say, that's a very convincing argument for why you shouldn't choose Pita!"

"Now hold on a sec!" says an old man in a Team Pita blouse, "That wasn't her message at all! The message is that only Pita is right for her!"

"You've heard the people, Bratniss!" says Coin. "And now, it's time for you to choose."

I pause for a second. "And what if I decided not to choose either of them?"

"I think it's obvious that we would kill you," calls out a young mom.

"Yes," says a teenage boy, not much older than me. "You would leave us no choice."

"Hi, there," says a small man in the back, "I'm actually one of the small group of people who want you to marry Mayor Undersee. But for this occasion we've allied ourselves with Team Pita, and we too agree that you must die if you don't choose one or the other. Probably in some sort of death tournament. Perhaps held next year, with winners from previous Games."

I glance over my shoulder at Pita and Greta. Pita has somehow gotten his hands on a stack of blueprint paper, and I can see him beginning to make detailed sketches under the heading "Ways to Use Evil Technology to Imprison Bratniss in an Even-Smaller Love Cave This Time." Greta, meanwhile, has managed to tie the earthworms Coin gave him into a circle. "*Holy circle of worms,*" he mutters. "*Prophecies have told of you. When placed on head, can man finally harness wormpower*?" Well, that settles it.

"Can I have some time to think it over?" I ask.

"Of course you can, dear," says Coin kindly. I walk over to the biker who killed that idiot who was all into *The Night Circus.*

"Do you mind if I sit on your bike's seat for a second? I find I do my best thinking while sitting down."

"Sure thing, baby," he says. [Note to reader: isn't that a cool way to show how a biker talks?]

Suckers, I think, a few moments later, as I toss the flaming motorcycle towards the crowd. In the confusion, I'm able to snag a different, nicer motorcycle. And with that, I speed away. I don't really know how to ride a motorcycle, but I'm sure I'll pick it up on the road. *Yes, that's what I'll do*, I think, during one of the many end-over-end crashes I keep making the bike have.

Suddenly, I hear a voice to my right. And, to my surprise, I see that the motorcycle has a sidecar I hadn't noticed before—and that Hagridmitch is in it!

"Hermione!" he says joyfully. "I a'fear'd that I'da never get to see ye again! Why, I've been stuck in here fer the entire tournament! Hang on now, because this motorcycle kin flyyyy-y-y-y," he says, tumbling out of his seat from the gentle push my hands give him. I watch in the side mirror as he rolls to a stop in a patch of sunflowers.

"Why, if it isn't *Minerva McGonogall*!" I hear him say to one of them, "Fancy meetin' ye here! What's that y'are askin'? Do I still recognize ye after all-a these years? O' *course* I recognize ye! I'd recognize ye anywhere, on account 'a yar face bein' made-a big black seeds n' all!"

And after that, I decide not to look back anymore. Because, hey, there's a whole post-apocalyptic world out there. And for once, I'm going to do exactly what I want. I'm not even sure what it will be, yet. Maybe I'll take some time to go break into old military research centers and play with their cool weapons. Or maybe I'll go start a war with some awesome new race of zombie-people. Maybe I'll even head up north to Canada. It's not the most exciting country, but at least they still have a functioning parliamentary democracy. Ah, who am I kidding, Canada would be way too lame. But the thing is, I don't need to decide what I want to do yet. When I find it, I'll know.

I smile to myself, and pat the shotgun I stole from Greta. *And I'll have this if anybody tries to make me do a sequel.*

The End

www.hungergamesparody.com
www.twitter.com/hungergamespoof
www.facebook.com/hungergamesparody

Made in the USA
Lexington, KY
03 February 2012